AF654001

7 SECRETS
OF THE
GODDESS

Devdutt Pattanaik writes, illustrates and lectures on the relevance of mythology in modern times. He has, since 1996, written over forty books and seven hundred columns on how stories, symbols and rituals construct the subjective truth (myths) of ancient and modern cultures around the world. He consults corporations on leadership and governance, and TV channels on mythological serials. His TV shows include *Business Sutra* on CNBC-TV18 and *Devlok* on Epic TV. To know more, visit devdutt.com

7 SECRETS OF THE GODDESS

DEVDUTT PATTANAIK

First published by westland limited in 2014

Published by Westland Books, a division of Nasadiya Technologies Private Limited, in 2022

No. 269/2B, First Floor, 'Irai Arul', Vimalraj Street, Nethaji Nagar, Alapakkam Main Road, Maduravoyal, Chennai 600095

Westland and the Westland logo are the trademarks of Nasadiya Technologies Private Limited, or its affiliates.

Copyright © Devdutt Pattanaik, 2014

Devdutt Pattanaik asserts the moral right to be identified as the author of this work.

ISBN: 9789395073073

10 9 8 7 6 5 4

The views and opinions expressed in this work are the author's own and the facts are as reported by him, and the publisher is in no way liable for the same.

All rights reserved

Typeset by Special Effects Graphics Design Co., Mumbai

Printed at Thomson Press India Private Limited

No part of this book may be reproduced, or stored in a retrieval system, or transmitted in any form or by any means, electronic, mechanical, photocopying, recording, or otherwise, without express written permission of the publisher.

I humbly and most respectfully dedicate this book to those hundreds of artists, artisans and photographers who made sacred art so easily accessible to the common man

Contents

Author's Note: On Reality and Representation ix

1. *Gaia's Secret* 1

2. *Kali's Secret* 43

3. *Gauri's Secret* 81

4. *Durga's Secret* 113

5. *Lakshmi's Secret* 157

6. *Saraswati's Secret* 203

7. *Vitthai's Secret* 227

Acknowledgements 259

Author's Note

On Reality and Representation

Lakshmi massages Vishnu's feet. Is this male domination? Kali stands on Shiva's chest. Is this female domination? Shiva is half a woman. Is this gender equality? Why then is Shakti never half a man?

Taken literally, stories, symbols and rituals of Hindu mythology have much to say about gender relationships. Taken symbolically, they reveal many more things about humanity and nature. Which is the correct reading? Who knows?

Within infinite myths lies an eternal truth
Who knows it all?
Varuna has but a thousand eyes
Indra, a hundred
You and I, only two.

On Capitalisation

Capitalisation is found in the English script but not in Indic scripts. So we need to clarify the difference between shakti and Shakti, maya and Maya, devi and Devi, goddess and Goddess. We may not always be successful.

Shakti is a proper noun, the name of the Goddess. It is also a common noun, shakti, meaning power. Likewise, maya means delusion, and Maya is another name of the Goddess. The word devi, spelt without capitalisation, refers to any goddess, while Devi, spelt with capitalisation, refers to the supreme Goddess. Often Mahadevi is used for the proper noun instead of Devi. Shiva may be Mahadeva, who is maha-deva, greater than all devas; similarly Shakti is Mahadevi, who is maha-devi, greater than all devis.

Without capitalisation, devi/goddess may also refer to limited forms of the female divine, while limitless ideas are referred to as Goddess/Devi using capitalisation. Ganga is devi, goddess of a river, while Gauri is Devi, Goddess embodying domesticated nature.

Context needs always to be considered. Kali is goddess in early Puranas, where she is one of the divine feminine collective; later she is Goddess embodying untamed nature. Saraswati seen alone is Goddess, but when visualised next to Durga, who is Devi, she becomes the daughter, hence goddess.

1. Gaia's Secret

Male anxiety is outdated

Greek mythology: Gaia, the earth-mother

Gaia is the earth-mother in Greek mythology. Her mate Uranus, the starry-sky, clung to her intimately and gave her no space. The only way her son, Cronus, could leave Gaia's womb was by castrating his father. From the blood drops arose Aphrodite, goddess of love, and the Erinyes, the goddesses of retribution, who were fiercely protective of the mother. Cronus then declared himself king and, to the horror of the Gaia, ate his own children to prevent them from overpowering him as he overpowered his father. Gaia saves one son, Zeus, from the brutality of Cronus, raises him in secret, and eventually Zeus attacks and kills Cronus. In triumph, Zeus declares himself the father of gods of men, takes residence atop Mount Olympus that reaches into the sky. Gaia remains the earth-mother, respected but distant.

This idea of a primal female deity, first adored, then brutally side-lined by a male deity is a consistent theme in mythologies around the world.

The Inuit (eskimo) tribes of the Arctic region tell the story of one Sedna, who, unhappy with her marriage to a seagull, begs her father to take her back home in his boat. But, as they make their way, they are attacked by a flock of seagulls. To save himself, Sedna's father casts her overboard. When she tries to climb back, he cuts off her fingers. As she struggles to get back in with her mutilated hands, he cuts her arms too. So she sinks to the bottom of the ocean, her dismembered limbs transforming into fish, seals, whales, and all of the other sea mammals. Those who wish to hunt her children for food need to appease her through shamans who speak soothing words.

Egyptian mythology: Nut, the sky-mother

The Tantrik tradition of India speaks of the primal one, Adya, who took the form of a bird and laid three unfertilised eggs from which were born Brahma, Vishnu and Shiva. Adya then sought to unite with the three male gods. Brahma refused as he saw Adya as his mother; Adya cursed him that there will be no temples in his honour. Adya found Vishnu too shifty and shrewd, so she turned to the rather stern Shiva who, advised by Vishnu, agreed to be her lover provided she gave him her third eye. She did, and he used it to release a missile of fire that set her aflame and turned her into ash. From the ash came three goddesses, Saraswati, Lakshmi and Gauri who became wives of Brahma, Vishnu and Shiva. Also from the ash came the grama-devis, goddesses of every human settlement.

Egyptian mythology acknowledges a time before gender. Then there was Atum, 'the Great He-She', who brought forth the god of air Shu and the goddess of dew Tefnut who separated Geb, the earth-god, from Nut, the sky-goddess, who gave birth to Isis and Osiris, the first queen and king of human civilisation. Then Seth killed Osiris and declared himself king, until Isis gave birth to Horus and contested his claim.

In these stories from around the world, the male deities compete for the female prize. This can be traced to nature, where all wombs are precious but not all sperms. So the males have to compete for the female. In many bird species, the female chooses the male with the most colourful feathers, the best voice or the best song, or with the capability of building the best nest. In many animal species, such as the walrus and the lion, the alpha male keeps all the females for himself; thus there are always 'remainder' males who do not get the female. This selection of only the best males creates anxiety amongst the not-so-good males and translates into

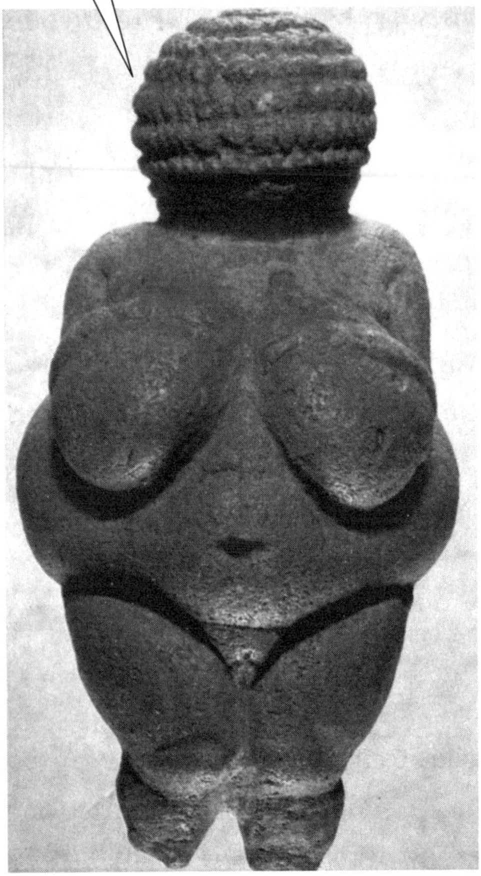

Stone Age Venus from Europe

Sacred ram from Mesopotamia

the fear of invalidation in the human species. To cope with this fear of invalidation, social structures such as marriage laws and inheritance rights come into being, often at the cost of the female.

As human society learnt to domesticate animals and plants, trade and build cities, we saw a gradual shift in social laws, deterioration in the status of women, and rejection of Goddess-worship in favour of God-worship.

After thousands of years as hunter-gatherers, humans learned to tame and breed animals. These pastoral communities valued all the cows but realised they did not need all the bulls to maintain numbers. Many bulls could be castrated and turned into beasts of burden, pulling carts and ploughs.

Could this apply to human society too? Not all males were necessary for reproduction. This is reinforced in the story of Nari-kavacha, whose name means 'he who used women as a shield', found in Hindu Puranas. When Parashuram slaughtered all the Kshatriya men, only one man survived by hiding in the women's quarters. From this 'cunning coward' sprang all the future Kshatriya clans.

That a tribe needed women, not men, for its survival manifests in Stone Age art where we find an obsession with fat, fertile female forms, or images of bejewelled women with their genitals exposed, while men are either reduced to the phallus or worshipped as the alpha bull, ram or goat.

This is the same reason why, in the Bronze Age, we find images of groups of women worshipped alongside a single male. Similar thoughts gave rise to the Yogini shrines found across India with

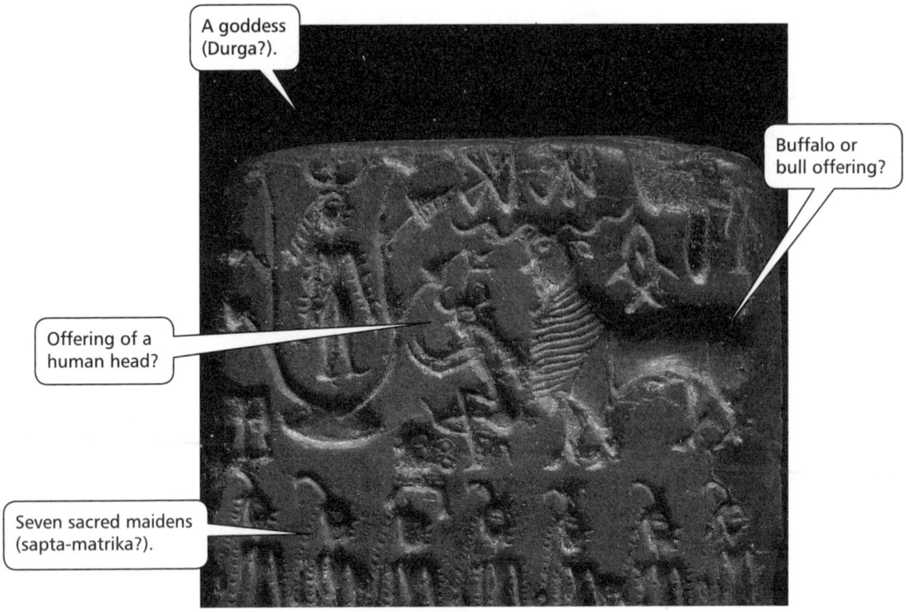

Indus seal showing goddess worship

Poster art showing self-sacrifice

Poster art of Hinglaj Mata of Balochistan

just one male, the Bhairava, and the practice of Kanya Puja, which involves worshipping a group of young girls accompanied by a single boy in north India during vasant navaratri or spring festival of the Goddess. A few anthropologists even argue that Krishna's raas-leela may have its roots in old matriarchal tribes where the women valued only one male of the village.

To get access to the women, men had to fight each other or simply submit to the woman's choice. This explains the origin of the 'swayam-vara' ceremonies described in the Hindu Puranas, designed to get the best male for the woman.

In such female-dominated cultures, the male could not refuse the woman: in the Mahabharata, when Arjuna refuses her advances, Urvashi curses him to turn into a eunuch. Any man who forced himself upon a woman was killed: in Greek mythology, Artemis turns Actaeon, the man who seeks to ravish her, into a stag that is ripped to pieces by his own hunting dogs. Anyone who attacked the man the woman chose would be put to death by other males: in Greek mythology, all the Greek warlords swear to protect the man Helen chooses as her husband. But there were always men eager to kill rivals and take their place as lovers: Greek mythology tells the story of Adonis, the boy-lover of Aphrodite, goddess of love, who is killed by the more virile and jealous Mars, god of war. These tales hark back to a pre-patriarchal, matriarchal, society.

To ensure that the dominant males did not have exclusive and eternal rights to women, the ritual of killing the chosen males at regular intervals emerged. The chosen one came to her during the sowing season and he was sacrificed at harvest season. The woman had no say in the matter. She could choose her lover, but her choice was fatal. The triumph of the dominant male was in fact a march

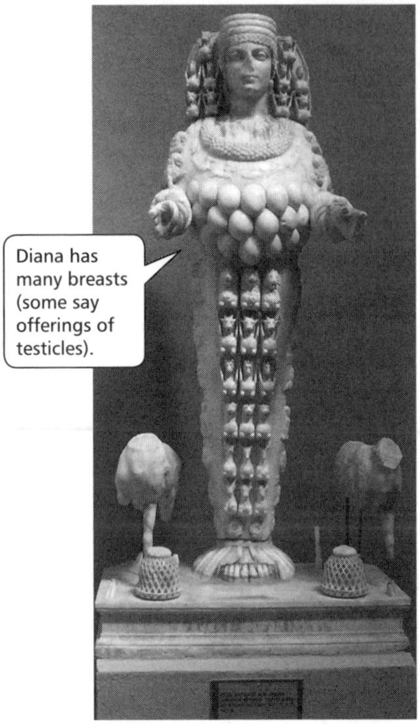

Diana of Ephesus

Ishtar of Babylon

Greek mythology: Adonis and Aphrodite

to death. So we find in Sumerian mythology, Innana mourning for her lover Dumuzi who comes to her every spring but departs in winter. In the *Rig Veda,* there is a hymn where Urvashi's husband, Pururava, pines for her while she leaves him for the realm of the gandharvas.

The only way to survive being killed at the end of the term as king and consort of the Goddess was by castrating oneself. And so in the Near East, the priests of Cybele, called the Galli, ritually castrated themselves emulating Attis, the castrated son/lover of the goddess. Some anthropologists trace similar thoughts to the practice of male priests dressing up as women and carrying pots during the worship of many grama-devis, the village goddesses of India.

We can speculate if the male heads around Kali's neck are the heads of men who were killed after they gave a child to the goddess of the tribe: an indicator of the price paid by the male sexual gaze. In Vaishno-devi, the Goddess is a virgin who kills the Bhairava for approaching her sexually, but then, after beheading him, she asks her devotees to worship him too. We can only speculate if this can be traced to the ancient rejection, or subjugation of the male sexual gaze.

It was perhaps at this phase of human culture that the Goddess came to be addressed as virgin mother, an ironical phrase it seems today, for how can a virgin bear a child? Today a virgin is a woman who has never had sex. But earlier it meant a woman who was ready to bear a child. Every woman then was a virgin between menstruations at the time of ovulation. This virginity was restored after childbirth. This thought informs a detail in the epic Mahabharata, where the heroine Draupadi walks through fire to restore her virginity before she goes to the next husband.

Polynesian mythology: Maui and Hine

We also find the virgin being referred to as a whore, which means a prostitute. This is a pejorative term today but long ago, before the idea of property became the cornerstone of human culture, it simply meant a woman who was free to go to any man. She was like the earth that accepts seeds from all plants freely; she was no field where the farmer controls the sowing and claims the harvest.

Over time, meanings changed and 'virgin' became a word of praise while 'whore' became an insult. The shift in meaning reflects a shift from an older time when women were free to a later time when women were bound to men.

▽

The close association of women with sexual pleasure and childbirth on one hand and death on the other is made explicit in the stories of Yama and Yami, the first living creatures in the *Rig Veda*. Yami, the sister, approaches Yama, the brother. He rejects her advances on moral grounds and eventually dies and finds himself trapped in the land of the dead as he has left no offspring behind in the land of the living. Thus, rejection of sex turns him into the god of death. Yami mourns for him, turning into the goddess of the night, Yamini, as well as the mournful dark river, Yamuna.

Similarly, in Polynesian mythology, Maui tries to get immortality for humanity by entering the vagina of Hine, goddess of death and the netherworld, traversing her body and leaving it by her mouth. But just when he enters, she wakes up and, realising what Maui is trying to do, bites him with the teeth she has lining her vaginal lips. Even in Greek mythology, humanity is at the mercy of goddesses known as Graces or Fates who spun the thread that determined the quality and length of everyone's lives.

Biblical mythology: Samson and Delilah

This connection of death with sex, sex with pleasure and pleasure with women resulted in men associating women with immorality, misery and vulnerability. Rejecting women through celibacy offered physical strength. In the Bible, Samson loses his hair and his strength when he succumbs to the charms of Delilah; he regains it when he rejects her and turns to God. Rejecting women granted freedom from suffering. In Buddhism, the daughters of Mara, god of desire, are associated with decay, disease and death; in rejecting them, Gautama Siddhartha of the Sakya clan finds freedom from suffering, and comes to be known as Buddha, the enlightened one. Rejection of women even granted liberation from death. In the Tantra we hear how semen shed into a womb creates the son but weakens the father; however, if one is able to achieve urdhva-retas, reverse movement of semen up the spine towards the head, one can get siddhi, magical powers to control nature, even outsmart death. These ideas led to the rise of monastic and mystical cults that sought to either control nature or escape from it.

To get celibate ascetics to marry, or at least produce children, the idea of ancestors arose, in China and India, obligation to whom forces a man to have children before he renounces the world. In the Puranas, these 'pitr', who hang upside down like bats in the land of the dead, goad sages like Kardama and Agastya to look for wives and father children.

But getting a wife was not easy. The Puranas refer to Gandharva-vivah, where women chose their lovers, alongside Asura-vivah, where women were bought, Rakshasa-vivah, where women were abducted, and Pisacha-vivah, where women were made pregnant while they slept.

These stories suggest the rise of trading communities, where

Kalamkari print of archery contest for the hand of Draupadi in marriage

Poster of Krishna abducting Rukmini

women became popular commodities with high demand and low supply, forcing men who did not have the qualities to attract or the wealth to buy, to turn to abduction, even rape, to secure wives. In the *Bhagavata Purana,* Krishna has to tame wild bulls to marry Satya, daughter of Nagnajit. In the Mahabharata, Bhisma abducts Amba, Ambika and Ambalika in order to procure wives for his brother, Vichitravirya. They were embodiments of wealth and power, mediums to create the next generation.

If pastoral society gave greater value to the stud bull while castrating the rest, if trading society started valuing the female as a commodity in great demand, then agricultural society introduced the idea of ownership.

At first, both men and women owned their bodies and so traded it freely. We hear of sacred prostitutes in Levant (Near East) and Babylon (Mesopotamia) dedicated to love-goddesses such as Astarte and Mytilla. The prostitutes were mostly women, but included a few men who were described as effeminate, or even castrated, known as catamites, who existed for the pleasure of men.

One reason given for the rise of sacred prostitution is that men took over all the economic activities of society, from animal husbandry to farming to trading, leaving women with no choice but to trade their bodies for pleasure and their wombs for procreation. Prostitute became a pejorative term as only the rich could afford the most beautiful of women. Gradually the word was used for all women who freely chose and discarded her lovers for a price. Eventually it came to be associated with exploitation, as women were denied ownership of their bodies. The woman's body, like

Roman mythology: Rape of the Sabine

the land, belonged to the father, brother, husband and even son. She was reduced to being just the field; man was the farmer, owner, customer and abuser. Her child now belonged to a man, either her brother in matrilineal communities or to her husband in patrilineal communities.

With fathers claiming ownership over daughters and deciding who she should marry, the practice known in Sanskrit texts as 'swayam-vara', where women chose their own husbands, came to an end. We find, in the *Bhagavata Purana,* Rukmini choosing to elope with Krishna rather than marrying the man, Shihupala, chosen by her father and brother. Likewise, in the Mahabharata, Subhadra chooses to elope with Arjuna, the man she loves, rather than marry the man chosen by her brother Balarama.

The Puranas speak of a Prajapati-vivah, where a man approaches the girl's father for her hand in marriage on grounds of merit. A Brahma-vivah is one where the girl's father offers her hand to a worthy man with the promise of dowry. In Deva-vivah, she is payment for services rendered by a man. In Rishi-vivah, a sage is given the daughter as a charitable gift, along with a cow (source of food and fuel) and an ox (beast of burden) so that he can become a householder. In the Mahabharata, Yayati gives his daughter Mamata to a priest who passes her on to four kings because it has been foretold she will be the mother of four kings. In exchange, each king gives the priest horses. Thus the priest is able to fulfil his promise to his teacher with the help of Yayati. No one asks what Mamata wants. But she forgives her father and retires to the forest.

In Nepal, until recently, women were dedicated as 'deukis' in temples. They had to take recourse to prostitution in order to survive. Many believed sex with deukis would cure them of many

The fierce and independent Bhagavati of Kerala

Devadasis who were dedicated to the temple deity

ailments. Children born to them have neither caste nor inheritance, as everything comes through the father. Similar practices have been traced to many parts of India, such as the mahari in Odisha and kalavant or deoli in Goa. These women were also associated with art and entertainment as they used song and dance to attract potential customers, and the relationship was not always sexual. The Sanskrit word 'devadasi' came into prominence only in the 19th century, when reform movements sought to outlaw these 'sacred prostitutes'.

Men wanted to 'own' their wives as they owned fields to ensure the child she bore was their child and not someone else's. Kunti states in the Mahabharata that at one time women were free to go to any man they pleased. Gradually their movements were restricted after Shvetaketu found his mother in the arms of another man and realised he may not be his father's son. Shvetaketu created marriage laws, limiting the number of men a woman could go to, and those only with her husband's permission. The Mahabharata limits the number of men a woman can go to as four, which is why Draupadi, who has five, is called a whore in the gambling hall by the men of the time. Significantly, in Vedic marriage rites, a woman is given to the moon, then to Gandharva Vishvavasu, then fire, and eventually her husband, thus forfeiting her rights to have more husbands.

In the Mahabharata, when Vichitravirya dies, his widows go to Vyasa in order to bear sons. Though biologically the children are Vyasa's, legally they belong to Vichitravirya. Thus the crop belongs to the owner of the field and not to the landless labourer who ploughed the field and sowed the seeds. Likewise, the five Pandavas are called children of Pandu even though he never makes his wives pregnant.

Greek mythology: Leda and the swan

Restricting the number of men a woman had access to ensured even the 'remainder' men of the tribe could get wives. But there was always the fear of being cuckolded by the wife, and of 'lesser' men ending up fostering the children of the dominant males. In Greek mythology, Zeus, king of Olympian gods, often seduces the wives and daughters of kings in secret. He takes the form of a swan and makes love to Leda. He takes the form of a beam of sunlight and makes love to Danae. He makes love to Alcmene by impersonating her husband, Amphitryon. In Hindu mythology, Indra makes love to Ahalya by impersonating her husband, Gautama. In the Ramayana, the sexual prowess of Ravana is constantly described leading to street gossip in Ayodhya as to whether Sita was truly chaste while held captive in the rakshasa's palace.

Further, there was great fear of a woman's 'excessive' sexual appetite. The Mahabharata tells the story of one Bhangashwana who was cursed by Indra to live half his life as a man and half his life as a woman. When asked what he preferred, he said a woman's life because the sound of 'mother' is sweeter, and because a woman has greater pleasure during sex. A similar story is found in Greek mythology where the seer Tieresias has lived life both as a man and a woman, and when Zeus asks him who gets greater pleasure during sex, he answers woman, angering Hera, wife of Zeus, who takes away his eyesight.

Fear that they would never be good enough to satisfy their wives, and that their wives would therefore find any excuse to seek another, more worthy lover, led to the imposition of strict laws on fidelity. Thus rose the Hindu concept of 'sati'. A wife's fidelity gave her magical powers, or 'sat', and made her 'sati'. For example, Renuka was so faithful to Jamadagni that she could

Sati shrine in Rajasthan

collect water from the river in unbaked pots made from riverbank clay. Sita proves her fidelity by going through a trial by fire.

A sati's fidelity allegedly offered her protection from widowhood. The Puranas tell the story of one Shilavati who carries her leper husband on her shoulders as he cannot walk. She satisfies all his desires. She even takes him to prostitutes. A sage is so disgusted by the husband that he declares he will die when the sun rises next. Shilavati then uses her power of chastity to prevent the sun from rising.

Belief in sati meant a widow was seen as a woman who could not prevent the death of her husband. To prove her chastity, she was encouraged to burn herself on her husband's funeral pyre, giving rise to the terrible practice of Sati and the worship of women who immolated themselves.

If rural cultures valued fertility, urban cultures valued obedience, for it indicated control and discipline. While fertility was rooted in women, obedience was enforced through men. With urbanisation came more rules and the idea of evil, one who does not submit to the rules. We find women at the receiving end of the rules, suggesting the city was a masculine invention.

This is explicit in Chinese mythology, where two natural forces work in harmony to create life: yang and yin. The masculine yang is like a dragon in the sky. The feminine yin is the earth, which like the phoenix rises from its own ashes, regenerating itself. There is no superior or inferior force in nature, say Taoist traditions, but in Confucian traditions, which favour culture over nature, hierarchy emerges, where the man becomes more important. The Emperor

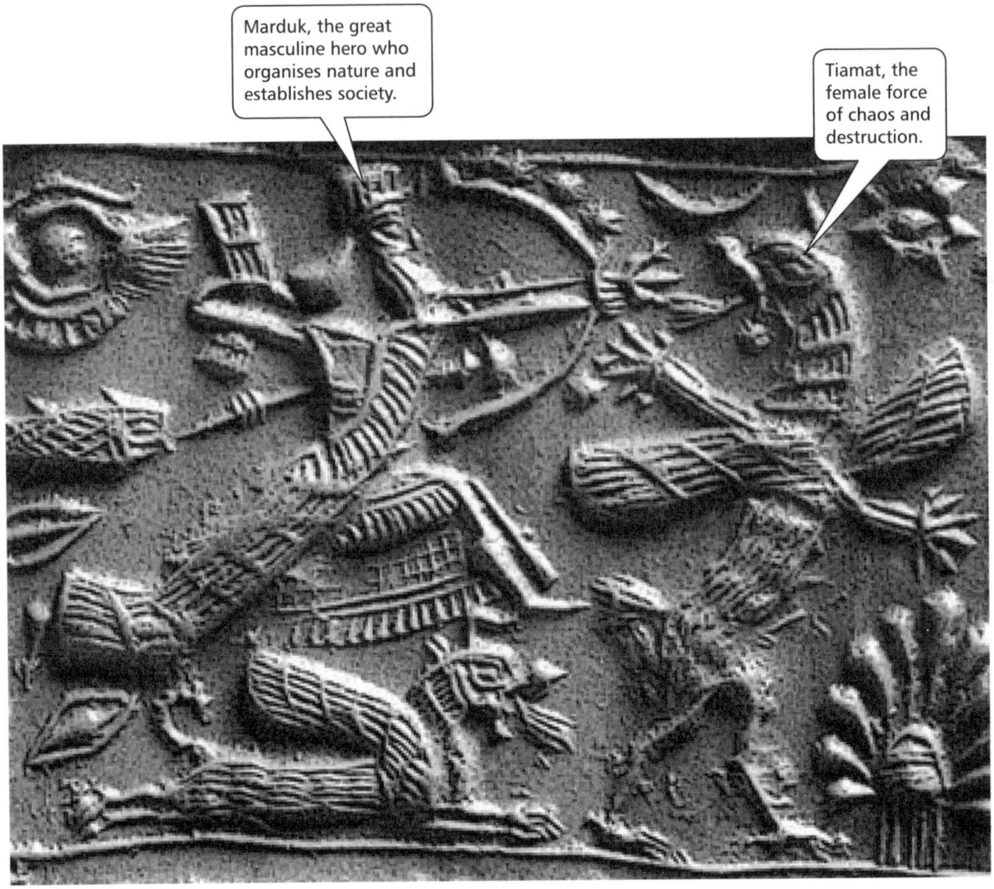

Mesopotamian mythology: Tiamat and Marduk

is given the Mandate of Heaven to sit on the Dragon throne in the Forbidden City, and asked to domesticate the earth, bring order where there is chaos.

A patriarchal society links women with nature and men with culture. Just as culture domesticates nature, men are asked to domesticate women. This is explicit in the Mesopotamian epic, *Enuma Elish,* where the god-king Marduk defeats the primal female monster Tiamat and brings order to the world. It is also explicit in Greek myths of Zeus chasing and raping nymphs across the land and fathering offspring.

In Japanese mythology, the first man Izanagi and the first woman Izanami stir the oceans to create the islands of Japan. They build a house with a pillar and go around it in opposite directions with the intention of copulating when they meet. When they meet, the woman speaks first and deformed demons are born. They go around once again and this time the man speaks first when they meet, and normal humans are born, thus establishing the need to make women subservient to men.

The battle of sexes found in Japanese mythology continues into the next generation. Izanagi's daughter, Amaterasu, the sun-goddess, born of his right eye, shares the sky with her brother, Tsukuyomi, the moon-god, born of his left eye. But then Tsukuyomi strikes the goddess of earth in disgust for producing food from all her orifices, including nose, rectum and mouth. So Amaterasu refuses to see him, resulting in the division of night and day, with the night belonging to the moon-brother and the day to the sun-sister. Amaterasu also competes with her other brother, Susanoo, the storm-god. He produces five men using her necklace and she produces three women from his sword. He says he won as he produced more offspring, but

Japanese mythology: The primal twins

she says she won as his sword produced women and her necklace produced men, thus inadvertently admitting that male offspring are of superior value to female offspring.

In cities we find the battle of power, the desire to be king, the competition between men, the younger lot seeking to overthrow the elders and the elders always suspicious of the youth. Women are the trophies of this masculine rivalry. They are seen as dangerous forces who seem to value desire over rules. Everyone is told to be wary of them.

In Greek mythology, for example, Zeus, fearful of human heroes, sends a box to Pandora, a woman, with a warning never to open it. She disobeys and out pours all the problems of the world that promise to keep humanity too busy to bother with trying to overthrow the Olympians. From that day, men are advised to be wary of all women; they were deemed the source of all problems in life. Not surprisingly, Greek democracy valued only men, and excluded women.

In biblical mythology, the woman Eve is tempted by the serpent to break the law of God by eating the fruit of the tree of knowledge, and compels Adam to do so too. For this act of transgression, both Adam and Eve are cast out of Paradise and Eve is made subservient to Adam. Before the creation of Eve, God is said to have created Lilith, of hairy legs, but she refused to be subservient to Adam and so was cast out: she became the mother of monsters.

As walls were built around cities, and wealth hoarded, urban centres often found themselves at war and under siege, surrounded by hungry tribes from the countryside who wished to tear down

Greek mythology: Pandora

Greek mythology: Furies chasing Orestes

their walls and claim what was hidden. In this world, a man was valued by what he had, women included. The raiders were keen not just to possess the wealth of those who lived behind the walls, but also their women. This led to increased isolation of women 'for their own good'. They were restricted to inner courtyards, and forced to go under the veil. Higher the social status, greater the isolation. Greater the isolation, the more valuable and desirable a woman became. Thus we find the concept of the virginal Snow White in European folklore, and a-surya-sparsha or 'untouched by the rays of the sun' in Indian folklore.

Society located its honour in a woman's body. And so a thousand Greek ships sailed to bring back Helen, wife of Menelaus, king of Sparta, who eloped with Paris, prince of Troy. Her action, say the epics, brought shame to all of Greece. After Troy was torn to the ground, the wives of Trojan warriors were brought back to Greece as concubines. Agamemnon, the leader of the Greeks, who had sacrificed his daughter, Ipigeniah, to ensure good winds as they sailed to battle, returned with the Trojan princess Cassandra by his side. Agamemnon's wife, Clytemnestra, was so angry that she murdered her husband and his concubine.

Orestes, son of Agamemnon, avenged his father's death by killing his mother, and her lover, Aegisthus. For the crime of killing his mother, Orestes was pursued by the dreaded female spirits known as Erinyes (also known as Furies) until Athena, goddess of good sense, intervened. She defends Orestes, and appeases the Erinyes by declaring them as goddesses of justice. This story reveals a shift from matriarchy (when the lover of the queen was ritually murdered and killing the mother was the greatest crime) to patriarchy (when killing women who challenged male authority

Biblical mythology: The rape of Dinah

and dishonoured the family was justified).

The Hebrew Bible tells the story of Dinah, daughter of Jacob, leader of nomads, who was abducted and violated by a Cannanite prince, who so wanted to marry her that he was even willing to circumcise himself so as to be an acceptable groom. This suggests the abduction was perhaps elopement and violation was perhaps intimacy by mutual consent. The brothers of Dinah did not think so. They killed the Cannanite prince while he was sore following the circumcision, and then they go on to plunder his lands, to the horror of their father, Jacob, who does not desire this enmity with the city folk. But the brothers argue, 'How can we let him treat our sister as a harlot?'

This assigning of honour to women plays out elaborately in the Indian epics. In the Ramayana, after Ram rescues Sita from the clutches of Ravana, he says, 'I rescued you not because you are my wife but to protect the honour of my family into which you married.' In the Mahabharata, the Kauravas publicly denigrate Draupadi by seeking to disrobe her only to humiliate her five husbands, the Pandavas. In these stories, the woman stops being a person; she is dehumanised and turned into a symbol of masculine honour. This transformation from prized possession to venerated object marks the triumph of patriarchy.

Excessive urbanisation also resulted in disgust for all things material. Meaning was sought beyond the city walls: in the untamed earth below and the open sky above.

Those who looked at the earth below saw it as the Goddess, manifesting in pairs and triads, embodying the paradoxes of the

Greek goddess triad of the Fates

Shift from earth to sky

world. There was Ishtar, the fertile, and Ereshkigal, the barren, in Sumerian mythology; Kali, the wild, and Gauri, the domestic, in Hindu mythology; the cow Hathor and the lioness Sekhmet of Egyptian mythology. In Greek mythology, there are the Fates triad who spin thread, the length of which determines the duration of human life, and the Grace triad who constitute the three seasons of spring, summer, and winter. Thus, the world is seen in feminine terms.

But gradually, the gaze turned upwards towards the sky. Gravity became a fetter, the earth a trap, and women bondage. Escape was sought. The serpent, messenger of the goddess, was rejected in favour of winged beings or angels who take humanity to 'higher' realms, above the earth.

In biblical mythology, the serpent becomes the symbol of the Devil, he who disobeys and tempts others to disobey. God, who makes all the rules, becomes male and resides in the sky. Prophets carry his word to earth. They are mostly male: Abraham, Moses, Jesus, Muhammad. They overshadow the few female prophets: Miriam, Deborah and Anna.

For Christians, Jesus is the son of God. There is no mention of a daughter of God. Mary was voted, only in the Catholic tradition, as the Mother of God, an eternal virgin celebrated as she conceives immaculately; but she is no Goddess. There is talk of Shekinah, the female spirit of God, in occult Judaic traditions, but she is never given form. There are many Marys in the Bible but none of them become apostles, not even the three Marys who witness Jesus' crucifixion and are the first to know of his resurrection.

In Arthurian legends that became popular in medieval Christian Europe, woman is the damsel, symbol of purity, who has to be

Biblical mythology

constantly rescued by the knight in shining armour. She is also the dangerous witch. In fairly tales, she is the Sleeping Beauty who can be awoken only by the kiss of a Prince Charming. Monastic orders around the world sought liberation from this burden of taking care of women and the children they bore.

In Islam, there is a folk tradition of how the Devil tries unsuccessfully, to include in the Koran through Muhammad, a verse that makes the three goddesses of Mecca — Urs, Mannat, Lat — mediums to Allah. These were the infamous Satanic verses. Still the feminine makes her presence felt as the hand of the prophet's daughter, Fatima, which is a common talisman used for protection and warding off the 'evil eye'.

In Jainism, all the Tirthankaras who establish the bridge out of ignorance to wisdom are male. In some traditions, one of the Tirthankaras, Malli-nath, is female. His female body is the result of a demerit: in his former life he fasted more than his companions in illness, and he did not inform his companions about it. He rejects his female body, viewing it as a vessel of putrefaction.

In the early days of Buddhism, Buddha refused to include women in his monastic order until he saw his step-mother cry at the death of his father and realised women suffer as much as men. Early Buddhist traditions saw wisdom in intellectual terms only. But later Buddhism made room for the emotional. Compassion was seen to be as important as knowledge. And compassion took the form of a goddess called Tara. She appeared as a tear shed when Buddha heard the cries of the suffering. Buddha decided not to accept nirvana but work tirelessly as Bodhisattva to help other suffering souls. All Bodhisattvas are male. But then we do hear of Guanyin, the female Bodhisattva of China, whose presence gave

Buddhist mythology

solace to all the suffering souls in the land of the living and in the land of the dead.

Four thousand years ago, before the rise of Buddhism, Vedic Hinduism paid greater attention to devas or gods like Agni (fire), Indra (rain), Vayu (wind) and Surya (sun), over devis or goddesses like Ushas (dawn), Vak (speech) and Aranyani (forest).

Since two thousand years, after the rise of Buddhism, in Puranic Hinduism, the gods gave way to God (bhagavan, ishwar). But God could not be explained without the Goddess (bhagavati, ishwari). She was no supplement; she was an intimately inextricably linked complement. This value placed on the feminine has been attributed to the popularity and influence of village goddesses or grama-devis, who have been revered in settlements across India since the dawn of time, long before the Vedas or the cities of the Indus Valley civilisation.

Three sects emerged in this later Puranic Hinduism: two masculine, focused on Shiva and Vishnu, and one feminine, focused on Devi.

Shiva is the ascetic who attacks Brahma for coveting and trying to control Devi; he shuns worldly life until Devi transforms into Gauri and makes him a householder and father.

Vishnu is the householder who looks upon Devi as Lakshmi, goddess of auspiciousness and abundance; taking various avatars to enable Brahma and his sons to cope with Kali.

But Devi is divinity in her own right, independent as the earth, responding to the gaze of Brahma who seeks to control her, Vishnu who enjoys her and Shiva who withdraws from her. She is their

Tantrik mythology: Adya, mother of Brahma, Vishnu and Shiva

mother, daughter, sister and wife. She allows them to dominate but never lets them have dominion over her. She enables everyone to outgrow the anxiety that creates patriarchy as well as the anxiety created by patriarchy.

2. Kali's Secret

Nature is indifferent to human gaze

Kali of Kolkata's Kalighat temple

Kali is perhaps the most dramatic form of Devi in Hindu mythology. She is naked, with hair unbound, standing or sitting on top of Shiva, sickle in hand, with a garland of male heads around her neck, her blood-stained tongue stretching out.

Is that tongue directed at us? Or are we just witnesses? Does she give that tongue meaning, or do we?

To understand Kali, it makes sense to appreciate the rise of Devi worship in India. And for that we have to appreciate the transformation of Hinduism over four thousand years from the pre-Buddhist Vedic phase of Hinduism where rituals were more important than gods (devas), through the post-Buddhist Puranic phase of Hinduism when devotion to God (bhagavan) gained paramount importance, to the rise of colonial gaze and the native reaction to it.

During this journey we shall see how the idea of Kali is more ancient than the name and form that we today associate with her. We shall also see how Kali's tongue transformed from being a weapon, to the symbol of wisdom, to the symbol of shame.

Around 2500 BCE (Before Common Era, formerly known as BC, or Before Christ), a city-based civilisation thrived along the Indus and Saraswati rivers (the latter dried out by 2000 BCE). Here we find clay figures of naked but bejewelled women alongside images of clay bulls. The bulls represent untamed male virility. The women, with their jewels, are representations of nature that has been domesticated. Together they represent nature's fertility

Indus valley Goddess images

over which humans seek control for their material welfare. We do not find any Kali-like images, but we do find an appreciation of the conflict between the wild and the tame. These cities ceased to exist by 2000 BCE but their cultural practices continued to thrive and spread in the Indian subcontinent.

Around 1500 BCE, a cattle-herding people migrated from the Indus-Saraswati river basins to the Gangetic river basin. Their relationship with the Indus cities has yet to be resolved. Their hymns, known as the Vedas, reveal a great yearning for cows, horses, grain, gold and sons. With fire (Agni) as their medium, they invoke virile warrior gods like Indra, and other masculine denizens who reside in the sky, more frequently than earth-bound goddesses. But there is reference to one Nirriti, who is acknowledged but asked to stay away for the sake of health and prosperity. Her name means one who disrupts 'riti', or the regular rhythms of nature.

Around 1000 BCE, Brahmana literature that links hymns to ritual elaborates on the nature of Nirriti. She is described as dark and dishevelled, associated with the southern regions, which is traditionally linked with death. This Nirriti is often identified as a proto-Kali especially since Kali is often addressed in later literature as Dakshina-Kali, she who comes from the south, south being the land of Yama, god of death. Nirriti embodies the human discomfort with the dark side of nature.

In Jaiminya Brahmana, there is the story of one Dirgha-Jihvi, she-of-the-long-tongue, who licked away the soma created during a yagna, much to Indra's irritation. This soma gave everyone, the devas included, long lives, happiness and health. Indra sends a young man called Sumitra to overpower her. But Dirgha-Jihvi rejects the man as he has just one manhood, while she has

Chola bronze image of Kali

many vulvas seeking satisfaction. So Indra gives that man many manhoods. Seeing Sumitra transformed thus, Dirgha-Jihvi is much pleased. They make love. Pinned down during the act of sex, Dirgha-Jihvi is momentarily immobilised, giving Sumitra the opportunity to kill her. This is also identified as a proto-Kali due to the references to the tongue and unbridled sexuality. It reveals male anxiety before female sexual and reproductive prowess.

Around 500 BCE, Buddhism and other sharmana (ascetic) traditions — which rejected the materialistic obsessions of society — grew. Words like karma and moksha gained popularity. There was talk of meditation, and bondage, and freedom. The yagna gradually went out of favour.

It is at this time that the name Kali appears for the first time, in early Upanishad literature, but it is the name given to one of the many tongues of Agni, the fire-god. In later iconography, we do find images of Kali with flames for hair. One can only speculate if the flame called Kali is in any way linked to the Kali with flames for hair.

The post-Buddhist period saw the gradual rise of Puranic literature. This literature spoke of a single, all-powerful divine entity, or God, who came to the rescue of devotees. Different people visualised God differently. For some, the Supreme Being was Shiva, the hermit. For others it was Vishnu, the householder. And for still others, it was the Goddess, Devi. Each school of thought vied for supremacy. Accordingly, stories came into being of how Devi vanquished asuras that neither Shiva nor Vishnu could defeat. Amongst Devi's many manifestations were Kali and Kali-like goddesses.

Poster of birth of Kali from Durga's brow

Shiva, Vishnu and Devi, and their many forms, can be traced to Vedic literature, while others to grama-devas or village-gods of India, where oral traditions perhaps pre-date the oldest Vedic hymns. Appropriation of grama-devas into more mainstream codified religions was common in this period, and so it is not uncommon to find similar gods and goddesses in Buddhist, Jain and Hindu mythology that became more elaborate during this period.

The earliest stories of the Puranas are found in the epics, the Ramayana and the Mahabharata, dated between 300 BCE and 300 CE. In them, we find a goddess called Kalaratri appearing on the final night of the battle at Kurukshetra when Ashwatthama ruthlessly murders the sons of the Pandavas at night when they are asleep. In Tamil Sangam literature, composed around this time, we come across the Goddess Korravai with flames for hair, associated with battlefields. Both Kalaratri and Korravai are Kali-like goddesses associated with rage and violence.

From around 300 CE, when the early Puranas were put together, Kali appears as a discrete goddess. She is born from the locks of Shiva's hair along with her brother, Virabhadra, and together they attack and destroy Daksha's yagna. In the *Devi Mahatmya,* which is a part of the *Markandeya Purana,* she is born from Durga's forehead to kill the demons Chanda and Munda. The *Devi Mahatmya* also retells Kali's most famous tale involving her tongue.

An asura called Raktabeeja had obtained a boon from Brahma that if a drop of his blood (rakta, in Sanskrit) fell on the ground it would transform into a seed (beeja) and sprout a duplicate of himself. No deva was able to defeat Raktabeeja. Any attempt to strike him with weapons only made matters worse. So the devas

Miniature painting of Durga and Kali combating Raktabeeja

led by Indra went to Brahma, who expressed his helplessness and directed them to Vishnu. Vishnu also expressed helplessness and directed them to Shiva. Shiva also expressed helplessness and appealed to the Goddess. And the Goddess rode into battle in two forms. The first form was of the multi-armed Chandi on a tiger ready to do battle. The second was Kali of outstretched tongue. Chandi struck the many Raktabeejas with her weapons, beheading them. Kali drank each Raktabeeja's blood before it fell on the ground. Thus, no duplicate Raktabeeja was created and the asura was killed. The Goddess made a garland of the asura's many heads and wore them as adornment.

Around 500 CE, Tantrik literature began to be composed. Unlike the Puranas, which seemed more interested in the external world, and in matters such as devotion and pilgrimages, the Tantras were more interested in the occult and alchemy. Here we find Kali and Kali-like goddesses such as Tara, Chamunda or Chinnamastika appearing with increasing frequency as part of a collective of three, seven, nine, ten, sixty-four goddesses variously known as Tri-devi, Tri-ambika, Matrikas, Maha-vidyas and Yoginis. These collectives include benevolent and fecund goddesses alongside malevolent and morbid goddesses. While these goddesses are also mentioned in the Puranas, their nature is elaborated on in the Tantras, which reveals a deeper appreciation of nature, sex and violence.

These goddesses embody folk deities associated with wild and domesticated spaces, and were gradually incorporated into Puranic and Tantrik, even Buddhist, literature. In the Mahabharata, we hear of Shiva's son Skanda informing a group of such wild female deities that if they are not worshipped and respected they have the freedom to harm pregnant women and children. In Buddhist

Poster image of Kali with the Maha-vidyas

literature, we hear of a child-devouring female demon called Hariti who is transformed into a child-protecting female demon by the Buddha.

By 1000 BCE, Kali emerges out of the collective and starts being seen as an independent goddess. In the *Kalika Purana,* she is the perfect, most primal representation of the Goddess. Some addressed this Kali as Maha-Kali to distinguish her from other Kalis. What distinguished her from all other goddesses was her nakedness, her unbound hair, her thirst for blood, her unbridled lust, her outstretched tongue and her domination of a male form, identified as Shiva or Bhairava. She either had one foot on him, stood on him or sat on him. But he is not a demon she has defeated. He is identified as her husband, one whom she awakens. She is the Goddess who makes him God.

By this time, when Hinduism is marked by the rise of vast temple complexes, Devi is identified with nature, and Kali with the most primal form of nature, before culture and outside culture, unaffected by rules and opinions of humanity. She is power, raw and elemental, both venerable and frightening. Human society is created within her; she ultimately consumes human society.

It often becomes difficult to distinguish Kali from Kali-like goddesses in Puranic and Tantrik literature. They seem to belong to a single continuum.

Bhairavi is often linked to Kali. But while Kali is shown standing or sitting on Shiva, Bhairavi and Shiva are seen as a pair, either located in crematoriums or wandering in the wilderness. Shiva is called Bhairava. As a pair they invoke violence, sexuality and

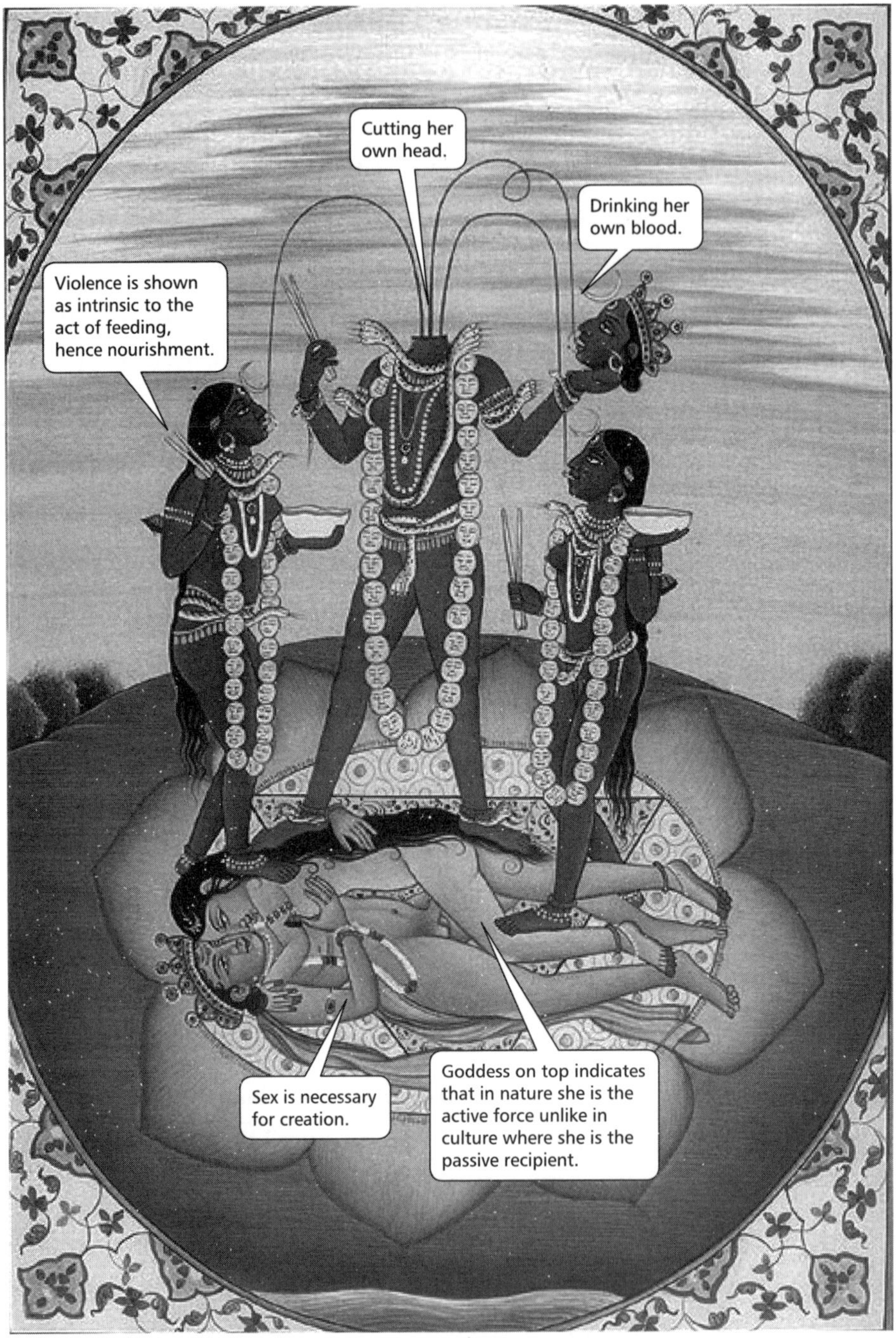

Miniature painting of Chinna-mastika

an indifference to social disapproval. Their images are also found on Jain temple walls indicating their popularity. Down south, Bhairava is often shown holding a human head. It is said to be the head of Brahma who dared seek to sexually dominate Bhairavi. In some tales this head cannot be placed on the ground and so Bhairava and Bhairavi take turns holding it; when they grow tired and place it on the ground, the world comes to an end.

Chinna-mastika means one whose head has been severed. She severs her own neck and her detached head drinks the blood spurting out of the neck. Thus she kills and nourishes herself, embodying that aspect of nature where the prey is killed to feed the predator. Thus in nature, violence becomes nourishment and contributes to survival. She also sits on Kama and Rati, god and goddess of desire, as they are copulating. Here, the woman is always on top of the man, indicating she is not the passive partner but the active one, initiating the sexual act, not simply the recipient of male passion. Here the sexual act is about procreation, not so much about pleasure, to keep rotating the cycle of life. Thus in nature, sex becomes procreative and contributes to survival.

Tara is indistinguishable from Kali, though they are named separately in Tantrik literature. She is both a Buddhist and a Brahmin goddess. Tara of Buddhism invokes compassion in Buddha and transforms him into Bodhisattva who delays his own liberation to help people out of the ocean of suffering. Likewise, Tara of Hinduism invokes compassion in Shiva and transforms him into a caring householder. In Bengal and Odisha, some distinguish Tara as the milder, more approachable form of Kali, one who need not be feared, one who can be invoked not only by hermits but also by householders.

Stone image of Chamunda

Chamunda is distinguished from Kali by her gaunt form. She is emaciated, sits on a corpse or a pile of corpses, and has a scorpion for her belly-button. This form seems to embody decay and drought. She is associated with dogs feeding on corpses either in the aftermath of a battle or an epidemic. She evokes despair and suffering.

As temples were built to enshrine Shiva, Vishnu and Devi, it became crucial to establish relationships between the three major deities of Hinduism. Shiva's ascetic nature connected him to to the wild forms of Kali. If she was nature that is indifferent to the mind (prakriti), he embodied the mind that is independent of nature (purusha).

In the more masculine Shaiva literature, nature is seen as passive, even subservient. Shiva enables the domestication of Kali on the request of Brahma and the other devas. Thus we have stories of how Shiva competes with Kali in a dance competition only to triumph over her by taking up positions that Kali is too embarrassed to assume. There are also stories where, by taking the form of a beautiful man or a cute child, Shiva is able to bind Kali by evoking marital and maternal desires in her. In this literature, the other does not exist. Nature, in particular, and all other living creatures in general, are but objects around the subject. Everybody and everything needs to be controlled.

But in the more feminine Shakta literatures, nature is active. Kali wants Shiva to pay attention to her for the benefit of humanity. Indifferent, he is no different from a corpse, or shava. In the less subtle Tantrik imagery, Kali does not merely step on Shiva, she sits

Bronze image of Shiva dancing

Stone image of Lajja-gauri

on top of him, intent on copulating with him. Only by engaging with her does he turn into Shiva, the auspicious one. Kali sits on top of Shiva, and gently coaxes him to make love to her, acknowledge her desires and satisfy her. She refuses to be invisible. This literature evokes the consciousness of man, the human ability to be sensitive and caring, the human ability to pay attention to the other. Here, nature is also a subject, as are others around the subject. Everybody and everything has a soul that needs to be respected.

Both Shaiva and Shakta literature tell the tale of how sages stumble upon Shiva and Shakti when they are making love. There are two versions of what follows.

In one version, the Goddess is shy. So she covers her face with a lotus flower. Shiva does not stop and so the rishis declare that Shiva would be worshipped only as a symbol, never in human form. This story explains the name Lajja-gauri, or shy consort of Shiva, given by male archaeologists to the clay image of the Goddess found in fields across India, where she is spread-eagled as if ready to receive a lover or deliver a child, and with a lotus for a face. It also explains why Shiva is worshipped as an erect stone (linga, or phallus) in a leaf-shaped trough (yoni, or womb) and rarely in human form.

In the other version, the Goddess is not shy. She simply sticks out her tongue, either in defiance of their disapproval, or in jest, amused that they seek to judge nature, for she is nature, unaffected by human opinions. Here Kali's tongue is a symbol that mocks the limitations, as well as the assumptions, of the human gaze. It reminds us that nature is sovereign. In nature, sex and violence ensure survival of the fittest. Human gaze judges sex and violence in ethical, moral and aesthetic terms. Be that as it may, humans have

Bhadra Kali, whose right foot is on Shiva

Smashan Kali, whose left foot is on Shiva

no choice but to submit to sex and violence in order to survive.

These two versions depict the conflicting attitudes towards sexuality that emerged in the post-Buddhist period, which saw the rising influence of monastic orders. In a similar vein, one finds, especially in Bengal, two forms of Kali. One in which she steps on Shiva with her left foot and raises a sickle in her right hand, and another where she steps on him with her right foot and raises her sickle with her left hand. The first one is seen as more fearsome and is called Smashan Kali, Kali of the crematorium. The second one is seen as more considerate of cultural norms and is called Bhadra Kali, Kali who is modest. The latter Kali was also called Tara, linking her to the compassionate Buddhist goddess. Smashan Kali is nature that ultimately consumes humanity. Bhadra Kali is nature that is understanding of human shortcomings. Smashan Kali is wild and free, beyond domestication. Bhadra Kali offers the strength to cope with the limitations of a domesticated life.

In Kali-kula Tantra, or Tantrik worship revolving around Kali, the point of eroticism was not indulgence or subversion, but a desire to confront one's deepest fears. It demanded that the aspirant break free from the social structures, customs and beliefs that offered him security. If he succeeded in doing so, he became vira, a hero. Confrontation with fears jolted the vira into wisdom. An encounter with Kali transformed a fool into one of India's greatest poets: Kalidasa, servant of Kali, who lived around the 5th century AD at the time of the Gupta kings, wrote extensively on unfettered love and longing in a world restrained by rules and hierarchies. Such a confrontation could also transform the vira into a rasa-siddha, he who knows the mysteries of alchemy. That is why Kali was also a venerated deity in the nath-sampradaya, a monastic

Poster art of Tarini, a local form of the Goddess in Keonjhar, Odisha order which originated around the 10th century, and was made up of wandering jogis who revered wise and powerful gurus such as Matsyendra-nath and Gorakh-nath. Similarly, legend has it that Krishnadevaraya, of the 16th century Vijayanagara empire, had a court jester called Tenali Raman who acquired his wisdom because he was amused rather than intimidated by the vision of Kali.

Since Kali was connected with Shiva, she could not be associated with Shiva's rival deity, Vishnu. The *Bhagavata Purana* tells the story where Vishnu in the form of Krishna fights a Kali-like goddess while she is defending Shiva's devotee, Bana, whose daughter, Usha, falls in love with, and abducts, Krishna's handsome grandson, Aniruddha.

And yet, the character most intimately associated with Vishnu's most popular avatar, Krishna, has all the characteristics of Kali, not in form though, but in thought. Her name was Radha.

From the 12th century onwards, Radha makes her appearance in the Hindu imagination in Prakrit works. But her popularity is traced to the 13th-century Sanskrit work, *Gita Govinda,* which describes in intimate detail her nocturnal and clandestine erotic dalliance with Krishna. The idea of gopis or milkmaids swooning over Krishna, leaving their homes in the dead of night and dancing around him to the tune of his music in the middle of the woods on the banks of the river, was known before the arrival of Radha. In the *Bhagavata Purana,* dated to the 12th century, there is no mention of Radha, but the rasa-leela is described to evoke various moods such as bhakti or devotion, shringara or eroticism, madhurya or tenderness, and viraha or longing created by separation. When

Miniature painting of Radha and Krishna intertwined

Radha appears, a new flavour emerges.

Unlike the gopis who are subservient and even admonished for being possessive, Radha is demanding. She quarrels with Krishna, and Krishna tries hard to appease her, even wearing her clothes sometimes, or falling at her feet. Unlike the self-contained hero of earlier works, he is distraught in Radha's absence. When duty beckons, and Krishna has to leave the village of Vrindavan and go to the city of Mathura, the gopis weep, but not Radha. Krishna promises that he will return but Radha knows he will not. When Krishna does not return and sends Uddhava to pacify the heartbroken milkmaids, Radha admonishes him for offering intellectual remedies for their emotional despair: she demands the right to feel frustrated and angry, but she does not begrudge her Krishna. She does not expect him to return. She describes him as a honey bee whose nature it is to go from flower to flower, but she, the flower attached to the branch of the tree, has nowhere to go but yearn for him and languish in memories and unfulfilled dreams and find validation therein. Thus she becomes the embodiment of true, unconditional, immersive love.

Later poets such as Vidyapati and Chandidas highlighted the scandalous nature of Radha's relationship with Krishna. She is described as a married woman in some songs, a woman who is older than Krishna in others, and in some oral traditions, his aunt, wife of Yashoda's brother. This makes the relationship extramarital, inter-generational and incestuous, breaking all boundaries imposed by society. This grants the nature of the relationship a very Tantrik theme.

Not everyone was pleased with such breaking of boundaries. There were fierce arguments about whether Radha was parakiya,

Miniature painting of Radha and Krishna in Madhuvan

belonging to another, or svakiya, belonging to Krishna. The folk traditions and regional literature were comfortable with the idea that Radha was married to another man, but in later Puranas such as *Brahmavaivarta,* concerted efforts are made to show how Radha and Krishna are two halves of the primal being, married in heaven but separated on earth. It reveals the discomfort with all things Tantrik commonly seen in mainstream society, and points to Radha alluding to Kali, despite being fully clothed.

It is interesting to note that Radha as an idea emerges after the arrival of Islam, which has been identified as the reason why Indian women, especially in the northern part of the subcontinent, started using the veil. Temples depicting Tantrik iconography were torn down to cater to the increasingly conservative mindset. Yet, Radha emerges, defying convention from behind the veil, leaving the inner courtyard to be with Krishna in the forest located beyond the influence of structures and hierarchies of the village.

The idea of Radha flourished primarily in the Gangetic plains. But it arose in the eastern areas of Odisha, Bengal and Assam, which were prominent centres of Tantra and Kali worship. Jayadeva, who wrote the *Gita Govinda,* lived near the Jagannath temple in Puri, Odisha, renowned for its temple dancers who were unattached to any man and were dedicated to the temple.

Later Radha's fierce love for Krishna would feature prominently in the devotional movement of Chaitanya to the extent that even men started identifying themselves with Radha, considering Krishna to be the only true, complete and perfect man. The psychological intensity of the romance was not mirrored physically; in fact, both the Chaitanya of Bengal and Shankardeb of Assam would celebrate continence and celibacy arising from true love for Krishna. Thus

Miniature painting depicting the rise of the Shakta cult

the overtly Tantrik traditions were tempered; yet, the idea of Kali who is indifferent to social conventions survived in the mind.

By the 15th century, the Ramayana*s* and Mahabharata*s* written in regional languages start associating their wronged heroines, Sita and Draupadi, with Kali. In the Adbhuta Ramayana, while Ram kills Ravana who has ten heads, Sita is able to kill a Ravana who has a hundred heads. In the Tamil Mahabharata, Draupadi transforms into Kali at night, running naked in the forest, eating elephants and buffaloes, as she is disappointed with her husbands, the five Pandavas. It is this Kali-side of Draupadi that makes her take the vow that she will wash her blood with the hair of the men who abused her. In fact, in these traditions, the story goes that Vishnu takes his various avatars such as Parashuram, Ram and Krishna only to satisfy the bloodlust of Kali, who wants to drink the blood of men who treat her with disrespect.

▽

While Tantrik rituals, where Kali played a central role, were known to many people, and Tantrik symbols could be found in villages across India, the meaning of the rituals and symbols remained esoteric. They were only known to those very few people who were steeped in Tantrik mysteries, people who were unwilling or unable to share their understanding in any coherent way with the masses, and who preferred to pass them on only to serious students and fellow practitioners. So it was only a question of time before Kali's association with Tantra resulted in her being situated outside cultural norms, where normal codes of ethics and morality did not apply. From a forbidding force she became a forbidden force.

There are stories, such as those in the *Katha-sarit-sagar,* which

Image of the mother of God that Europeans were exposed to.

Tantrik image of Kali decapitating herself while she copulates with Shiva; these kind of images shocked the sensibilities of Europeans who were unfamiliar with the occult symbolism and eager to believe the worst about the native 'savages'.

Clash of two worlds

dates to the 11th century, where sorcerers and thieves seek to invoke Kali and get powers from her by offering blood sacrifices at night in crematoriums. In medieval regional Ramayanas, such as the Adbhuta Ramayana written in the 15th century, we find the story of Mahiravan, king of the netherworld, a great magician, who, goaded by Ravana, tries to sacrifice Ram to violent and sexual Kali, but is outsmarted by the serene, celibate Hanuman.

When the Europeans came to India in the 16th century, they could not appreciate Kali's image, especially her nakedness and violence, so far removed from the images of the docile, virginal Mary and her son, Jesus, which they associated with God. In fact, Kali terrified them, endorsed their presumptions about the natives being savages. They became convinced Hindus were worshippers of the Devil, and indulged in human sacrifice. This was reinforced by medieval Sanskrit stories and plays where sorcerers sacrifice men, even women, to Kali in order to get magical powers. In the 19th century, army reports spoke of a band of highway robbers known as Thugees in north India, who worshipped Kali and offered her their victims as sacrifice in exchange for protection. Novels such as *Around the World in Eighty Days* reinforced this image of Kali, savage goddess of savage natives. It justified colonisation as the White Man's Burden to civilise.

Today scholars doubt whether this 'cult of murderous thieves' really existed or were the invention of a hyperactive colonial imagination eager to think the worst of those they were determined to subjugate. In all probability, the 'thuggee' were notorious thieves, driven by poverty not religious dogma, who worshipped Kali like everyone else around them. But the image of a murderous tribe inspired by Kali had such an impact that even today they inspire

How the West saw Kali in colonial and post-colonial times

tales not just in Hollywood (*Indiana Jones and the Temple of Doom,* 1984) but also in Bollywood (*Sunghursh,* 1968).

This colonial gaze embarrassed the natives of India, especially the young men of Bengal's privileged classes who were now being educated in English schools and exposed to European ideas. They re-imagined Kali's image differently.

In the 18th century Kali started becoming the object of devotion. She inspired poets like Ramprasad Sen and this created a new musical genre called Shyama Sangeet. Shyama means the dark-one, and is one of Kali's many names. Here, Kali was seen less in terms of power and more in terms of love. Despite her fierce form, which evokes fear and disgust, she was addressed as an affectionate mother who grants supreme wisdom to her helpless children in the most unconventional way: by denying them material pleasures and exposing them to the terror of existence. It is this Kali to which Vivekananda and his guru, Ramakrishna Paramhansa, allude. This devotion to Kali was clearly an extension of the larger bhakti movement that swept India from the 13th century onwards, but this was mostly focused around Shiva and Vishnu. Kali's transformation into loving mother in Bengali devotional literature, which seems to be in denial of her terrifying form, does indicate at one level an attempt to pacify the disapproving gaze of the colonial masters. At another level, it was perhaps born of the desire to explain human suffering: like the Bengal famine of 1770 resulting from the East India Company's excessive taxation policies that claimed the lives of ten million people.

In the tradition of Shyama Sangeet arose a very different story to explain Kali's tongue. It speaks of how Kali, after killing asuras, goes on a killing frenzy, intoxicated by the demon's blood. Terrified,

How Indians saw Kali in colonial times

all the creatures of the world beg Shiva to stop her. So Shiva throws himself to the ground in her path. She steps on him, realises she has stepped on her own husband, and is so embarrassed by her action that she bites her tongue. This makes Kali's outstretched tongue a symbol of embarrassment, even shame, as touching anyone with one's feet is a mark of disrespect in traditional Hindu households, especially the husband who was identified as pati-parameshwar, or the husband-God. This story is steeped in patriarchy. It views Kali's form as transgressive behaviour inappropriate for cultured women. It appealed to the sensibilities of those newly educated in European ways.

With the rise of the freedom struggle, many nationalists accepted the Western discomfort with Kali's image. But they gave it a different spin. Authors such as Bankim Chandra visualised Kali as Mother India, gaunt and naked and dishevelled because she has been reduced to poverty by the British rulers who oppress and exploit her.

In post-colonial times, with the rise of the feminist movement, Kali became an image of revolution and subversion. In her nakedness and refusal to submit to the male gaze, she became a symbol of women's freedom, both in India and abroad. She was seen to embody raw female energy before it was forced to conform to patriarchal norms. She was also seen as female energy that will ultimately triumph over masculine hegemony.

Increasingly Kali is becoming part of global neo-paganism and neo-feminism that seeks not to confront masculinity but embrace it in its fold. She is being seen as the embodiment of a woman's completeness and autonomy, which does not seek a man's gaze to define herself in anyway. In these movements, both men and

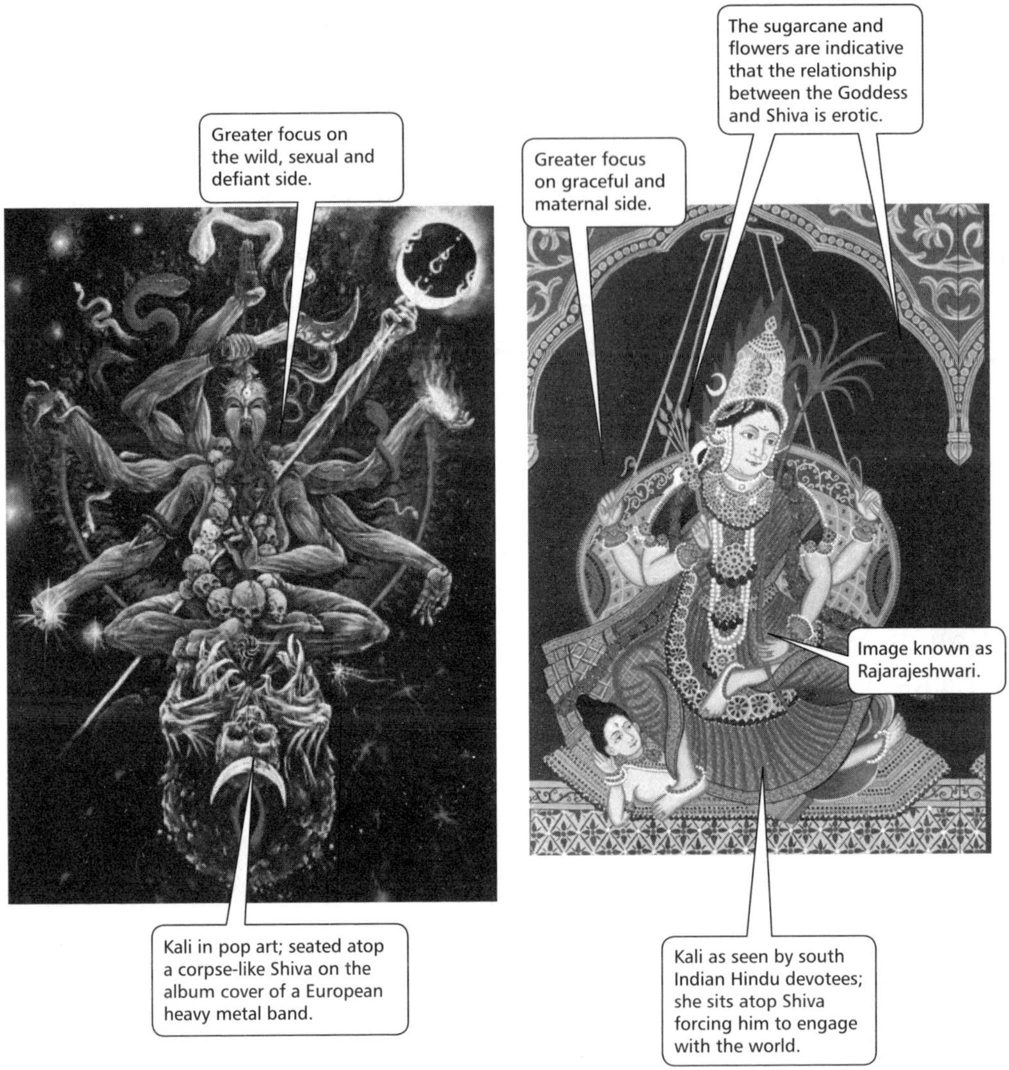

Two ways of seeing Kali

women are encouraged to break free from cultural conditioning, outgrow masculine anxieties related to hierarchy and validation, rediscover the elemental feminine energy of nature, and love life for what it truly is.

3. Gauri's Secret

Culture is dependent on human gaze

Calendar print of Jagadamba, the mother of the universe

Before humanity, there was only nature. After humanity came culture. In nature, only the fit survive and there are no favourites. In culture, even the unfit can thrive, but there are also favourites. Kali is nature, the mother: naked with hair unbound. Gauri is culture, the daughter, the sister, or the wife: demure and dressed with hair bound.

▽

The characteristic feature of Hindu mythology is the great emphasis on the mind, hence perceived realities.

In the Vedas, the poet or kavi wonders: What came first? Who came first? Was it water? Was it air? Was it the sky? Who witnessed their creation? Who can testify they came first? The gods? But are even the gods creations of the mind? What existed before the mind? Who created the mind? Can we ever know?

Later Vedic texts clearly distinguish between prakriti (nature), sanskriti (culture) and brahmanda (imagined reality of every individual). These are the three worlds we inhabit. The question persists: what came first?

Evolutionary biologists are clear that nature came first, then came the mind and only after that came culture. Life on earth began a billion years ago, but the human brain evolved only a million years ago; language, hence culture, emerged less than fifty thousand years ago. Thus prakriti came first, then Brahma (humanity), then brahmanda (Brahma's egg of thought), then sanskriti. Humanity however deludes itself that Brahma created prakriti first, then sanskriti.

Calendar print of Balambika, daughter of humanity

These ideas were expressed in narrative form in the Puranas. In these stories, the male form is used for the mind, while the female form is used to explain the material world around. The relationship between man and woman, or rather God and Goddess in the Puranas, serves as an allegory to explain the impact of the mind on the world and the impact of the world on the mind.

We are conditioned to assume that mind is superior to matter, hence the attribution of male form to the mind and female form to matter seems like yet another case of gender prejudice. The attribution, however, has more to do with biology: the male form lends itself best to represent the mind as the mind can express itself and affirm its existence only through matter, just as a man can only produce a child through the woman. Semen then, in mythic vocabulary, is a physical representation of thought that becomes reality (the child) through the woman (matter). When a sage spurts semen in the presence of a nymph, it does not mean a man being seduced by a woman; it means a quiet mind that has been provoked into thought by the events in the world around.

That being said, it is easier to read symbols literally ('Shiva is man and Shakti is woman') rather than symbolically ('Shiva is mind and Shakti is matter'). There is no escaping this.

The narrative in the Puranas begins with pralaya, a time marking the dissolution of the whole cosmos. Nothing exists then but waters that stretched into infinity. On the waters Vishnu sleeps, as on the coils of the serpent Sesha. So deep is his slumber that Vishnu is not aware of himself. This form of Vishnu is called Narayana. That is when the twin asuras, Madhu and Kaitabha, emerge out of Vishnu's earwax and create trouble. They steal the Vedas and create havoc. Who got rid of them? It was the Goddess, Yoga-nidra.

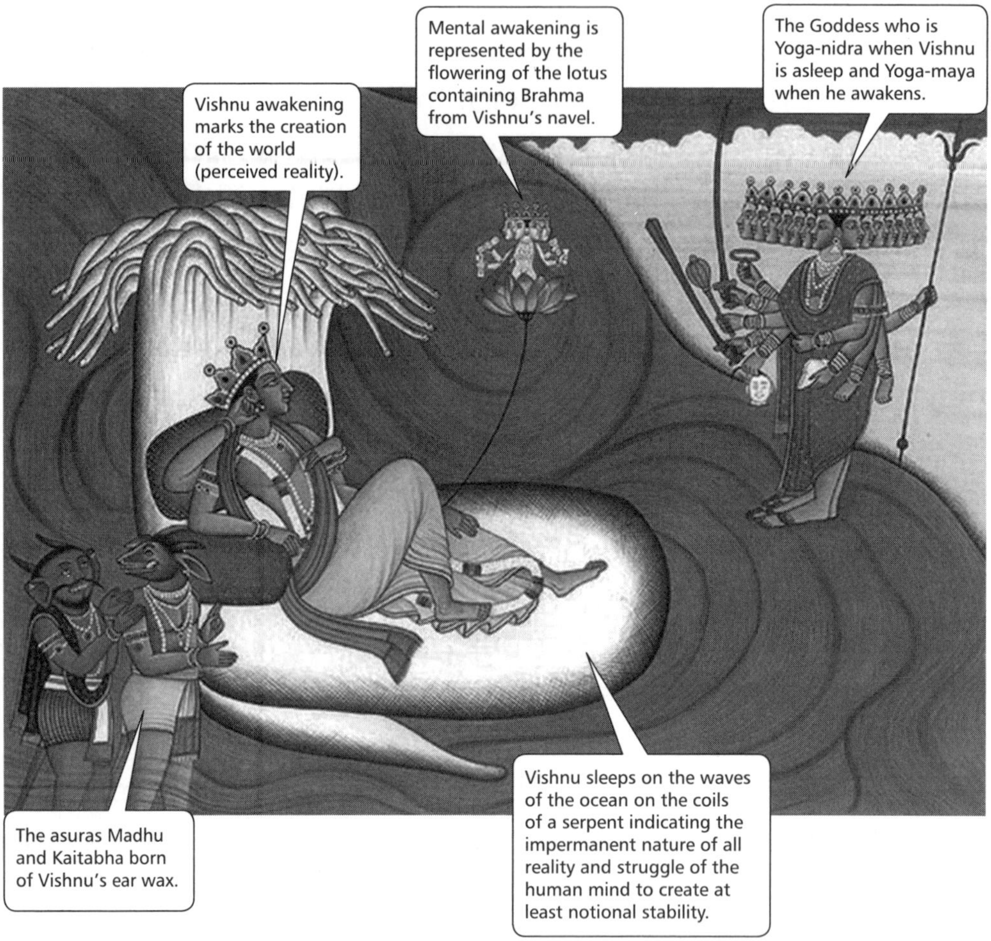

Pahari miniature of Yoga-maya

But how do we know? Was there a witness? Who was the witness?

It was Brahma, born of the lotus that rises from Vishnu's navel. He saw the birth of Madhu and Kaitabha, their theft of the Vedas, their killing at the hands of the Goddess, the dismemberment of their bodies, and finally the transformation of their body parts into continents. Brahma sang songs to Yoga-nidra's glory. Only, he called her Yoga-maya.

Narayana here is our sleeping mind, Vishnu is our awakened mind, while Brahma is our partially awakened mind. Madhu and Kaitabha are our thoughts emerging from the partially awakened mind. These are our negative thoughts, hence asuras, commonly (though incorrectly) identified as demons. Positive thoughts, come to be known as devas, commonly (though incorrectly) identified as gods.

The Goddess in this story is nature, present even when there is no human awareness. She is Yoga-nidra: nature witnessed by no one. She is also Yoga-maya: nature witnessed by an unenlightened mind. Yoga-nidra is reality but Yoga-maya is perceived reality, filtered through the human mind. Eventually, the mind will discover that she does not need him but he surely needs her.

What is the name of this perceived reality? She is called Adya, the primal one. She is called Shakti, the energy from which all things are created. She is called Maya, everything that the human gaze defines and evaluates. She is the mother, Kali. She can also be the daughter, Gauri.

Brahma, Vishnu and Shiva are commonly identified as the creator,

Calendar print of the trinity of the Puranas

preserver and destroyer. But what do they create, sustain and destroy?

The assumption is that they create, sustain and destroy nature. But nature, the Goddess, is swayambhu, self-created and self-contained, sustained by karmic laws. What is being continuously created, sustained and destroyed is perceived reality, the multiple impermanent forms of the Goddess.

That is why God-mind is associated with verbs: creation, sustenance and destruction. The Goddess-matter, by contrast, is associated with nouns: wealth, power and language, as Lakshmi, Durga, Saraswati. The God-mind draws wealth, power and language by organising nature into culture.

When Brahma, our unenlightened mind, perceives nature, he is unhappy as she is indifferent to his gaze and his views and his opinions. He seeks to control her. He creates culture by domesticating nature. For him, Gauri is daughter, who must obey him. By controlling her, he derives pleasure from her. This makes Brahma, the creator, unworthy of worship.

Shiva, by contrast, is indifferent to perceived nature. He is the tapasvin, the ascetic, who withdraws completely from nature. His mind has no notion of what nature is or should be. It is pure, clean, uncontaminated by thoughts. This is what makes him the destroyer of culture. Devi seeks to marry him, make him open his eyes, transform from the tapasvin Shiva who is withdrawn to the yogi Shankara who is willing to engage, so that he protects her from Brahma's bothersome gaze.

Shiva is embedded so deep in our consciousness that even we are not aware of it. The purpose of life is to invoke that hidden, unexplored potential. When Shiva awakens and acknowledges

Poster art showing Kamakhya

Shakti, Vishnu is born.

Vishnu is our wise mind capable of understanding perceived nature. Only he appreciates Kali and Gauri. He understands the insecurities of Brahma and the value of Shiva. He balances the two and so is the preserver of culture. For him, Devi is sister. She can also be mother, wife and daughter.

Symbolic readings of mythology are problematic for many reasons. Modern academic education is based on scientific principles as well as Euro-American bias that are more comfortable with the literal, the measurable, the singular and the objective ('this makes sense to all, so is true'). Indian readings of the Puranas tend to be highly individualistic and subjective ('what is sense for you may be nonsense to another and that is fine, for truth is plural'), hence there is room for multiple readings depending on the reader's intellectual capability. Each reading is valid.

From Brahma comes knowledge or Veda. This knowledge exists in the forms of poems called mantras, which are chanted during rituals called yagnas. Details about these yagnas are compiled in manuals known as brahmanas. The keepers of these brahamana texts were known as brahmins.

Killing these knowledge-carriers or brahmins was considered the greatest of crimes in the Hindu world as it meant the loss of Vedic knowledge that enabled humanity to turn nature into culture. However, every Purana tells the story of brahma-hatya-paap, the crime of killing a brahmin, committed by both Shiva and Vishnu.

The *Shiva Purana* tells us that when Brahma's daughter came into being, she went around her father as a mark of respect. But

Poster art showing the Goddess and her attendants

Brahma desired her. Disgusted by the incestuous cravings of her father, she ran away. He pursued her. Her disgust gave rise to Shiva, who beheaded Brahma and took upon himself the great burden of brahma-hatya-paap.

The *Vishnu Purana* tells us that Ravana, a brahmin, abducts Ram's wife, Sita, not remembering that she is actually his daughter whom he had abandoned long ago. Ram ultimately overpowers Ravana with the aid of a monkey called Hanuman, who chooses to stay celibate in the service of Sita and Ram. In this narrative, Ravana can be seen as Brahma, Ram as Vishnu and Hanuman as Shiva. Sita is the Goddess. While Shiva does not apologise for beheading Brahma, Ram performs austerities to rid himself of the demerit earned for his brahma-hatya-paap. For Vishnu understands the fears that make a Ravana behave as he does.

Images of the Goddess in north India are often flanked by images of Hanuman (also called langur-vir) and a childlike form of Shiva (Bhairav-baba) holding the severed head of a man, alluding to the tale of Brahma's beheading for looking upon Gauri with eyes of desire.

This narration of Brahma's incest can be seen literally as reinforcing a social taboo. It can also be seen historically as a reference to the end of the old Vedic culture of yagna that was eventually replaced by the later Puranic culture of puja. But it is more meaningful when seen symbolically and Brahma is recognised as the human mind that seeks control over perceived reality. This symbolic explanation clarifies why Brahma is not worshipped in any Hindu temple.

Brahma is the human mind that misbehaves. Shiva is the human mind that vehemently rejects this misbehaviour. Vishnu

Miniature painting of Bhairavi, the fearsome goddess

is the human mind that does not condone this misbehaviour, yet understands it.

What is this misbehaviour? It is the assumption of property: that culture and all its creation belongs to humans. This assumption is dependent on another assumption: that human value is dependent on property. Shiva, the hermit, rejects this assumption. Vishnu, the householder, traces the origin of this assumption to the human fear of validation. We do not know who we are and what the purpose of our life is, so we find solace in creating and hoarding property. That is why Brahma seeks dominion over Devi, while Vishnu and Shiva don't. That is why Brahma is unworthy of worship and that is why his ritual of yagna, described in the brahamana texts, that sought to establish human dominion over nature, was abandoned in favour of puja, where humanity is encouraged to adore Vishnu, Shiva and Devi.

Gauri is more commonly known as Parvati, wife of Shiva, daughter of Himavan, who is god of the Himalayan mountain range, also known as Parvateshwar, or lord of the mountains. She is also called Uma. In her previous life, she was Sati, daughter of Daksha, son of Brahma who established the yagna ritual. Parvati/Uma is the mother of Ganesha and Kartikeya. She is associated with the household. In folk tradition, and especially in Tamil temple lore, she is the sister of Vishnu. It is Kali who domesticates the hermit Shiva and in the process gets domesticated herself as Gauri.

The story is elaborated in the *Shiva Purana,* where Brahma, after being beheaded, feels that Shiva needs to get a wife. Yes, he went overboard in his relationship with his daughter but that is

Miniature painting of devas invoking the Goddess

no reason to reject culture and stay away from women. So Brahma consults Vishnu and they evoke the Goddess who promises to help by taking birth as the daughter of Daksha.

Daksha is associated with the yagna, a ritual based on exchange, which is the hallmark of human culture. Animals do not exchange; they grab what they want. Humans are capable of exchange. It forms the cornerstone of human society. During the yagna, Daksha makes offerings to the devas and expects gifts in return. He contributes in order to consume. He offers them his daughter and they, in turn, ensure that nature provides for all his material needs. He demands obedience from all his daughters and his sons-in-law for the sake of stability and predictability. He fears disobedience as he thinks it will herald the collapse of the structure he has created.

More than disobedience, Daksha fears indifference. The tapasvins ignore him and do not care about his yagna. They value tapa, mental fire churned by tapasya, more than agni, physical fire of the yagna. Tapa evokes thoughts that make a man wise; agni transforms things that make a man rich and powerful. Daksha despises the tapasvins.

So it comes as a huge shock for Daksha when his youngest daughter, and his favourite child, Sati, shows a preference for Shiva, the supreme tapasvin. When her father does not grant her permission to marry him, she simply leaves the house and follows the naked hermit. To teach her a lesson, Daksha conducts a grand yagna where he invites all his daughters and his sons-in-law, except Sati and Shiva.

Sati, as stubborn as her father, arrives at Daksha's doorstep anyway, despite Shiva warning her not to go, and demands to be treated as a daughter returning home should be treated. Daksha

Calendar print of Sati immolating herself

Calendar print of Bhadra-kali destroying the yagna

does no such thing. Instead he insults her and her husband explaining why he is not worthy of an invitation to the yagna. 'He follows no rules. He is covered with ash. He drinks poison and narcotics. He has no family or friends. Alone, he wanders naked in crematoriums in the company of dogs and ghosts. He is unfit for civilisation.'

Sati tries to explain to her father that Shiva is no rebel, but a hermit. He simply does not value himself through social structure, rules and property that indulge human hunger and fear. He performs tapasya and ignites tapa to outgrow hunger and fear.

But Daksha does not listen. For Daksha, unquestioning participation in the yagna is the only virtue. So angry is Sati at being unable to get through to her father that she leaps in the pit of fire in the ritual precinct and burns herself to death. Still the yagna continues, for Daksha refuses to be cowed down by his stubborn, defiant daughter.

When Shiva learns of Sati's death, his otherwise tranquil nature gives way to rage. He becomes Rudra, the howler. He tears out the locks of his hair and strikes them to the ground. Out come the sword-wielding Vira-bhadra and Bhadra-kali, manifestations of his outrage. They storm into Daksha's house, disrupt the ceremony, drive away the devas and ultimately behead Daksha.

But when the yagna stops, civilisation ends. Vishnu appeals to Shiva and begs him to restore the yagna by bringing Daksha back to life. Shiva does that, for he has no problem with the ritual itself, his problem is only with the assumptions and attitude of Daksha who seems to repeat Brahma's primal incestuous misbehaviour. Finally, Daksha is given an animal head, that of a goat, a reminder that a more worthy offering in a yagna is his own desire to dominate and

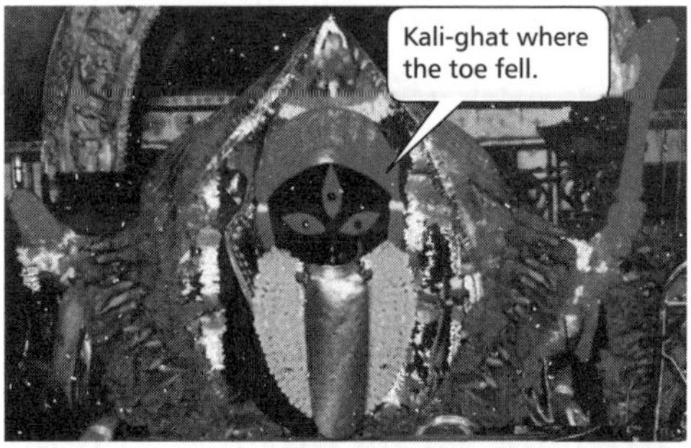

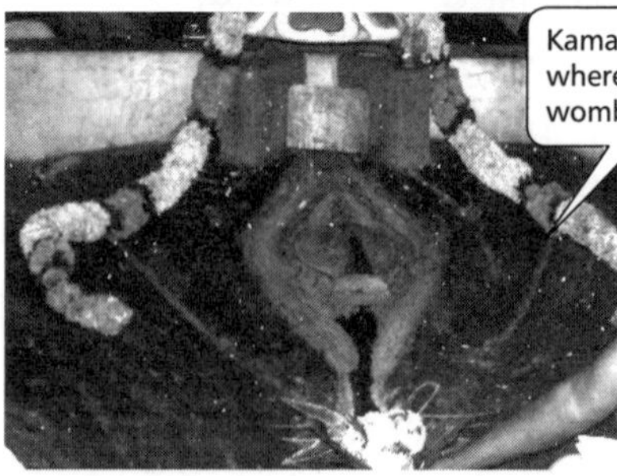

The Shakti-peethas

control the world like a dominating alpha goat.

Shiva then picks up the charred lifeless body of Sati and wanders the world, weeping. No more is he the detached hermit. He is now the lover inconsolable in his loss. His pain and suffering disturb the gods who beg Vishnu to put an end to it, for all things have to end, even bereavement. So Vishnu cuts Sati's corpse into tiny pieces. These fall in different parts of the world and became Shakti-pithas, centres of Goddess worship.

With Sati gone, Shiva shuts his eyes and resumes his meditation, withdrawing all attention from the world, generating inner fire and creating a cold, icy, desolate landscape around him.

Eons pass before the devas remember Shiva and want him to open his eyes, marry and father a child. For they are in trouble. Their paradise has been attacked by asuras. The devas need a commander to lead their armies. Their king, Indra, is not capable, for the leader of the asuras can only be killed by a warrior-child. Such a child can only be produced by a man who has been celibate for a long time. In other words, Shiva.

But when the gods send Kama, the god of desire, to strike Shiva with his arrows that arouse the senses, Shiva opens his third eye and lets loose a missile with his glance that sets Kama aflame and reduces him to a pile of ash. So the devas turn to the Goddess once again. And she promises to help, becoming Parvati, the daughter of the mountain-god, Himavan.

Parvati makes Shiva open his eyes and marry, but very differently. Unlike Sati, she does not follow Shiva. Unlike Kama, she does not arouse him sexually. She simply prays to him by

Chola bronze of Tapasvini Parvati

refusing to eat, drink or move, thinking only of him, resisting all temptations, until he is forced to appear before her and give her what she wants. Shiva finally appears and agrees to come to her house as a groom comes to receive his bride.

Shiva, unaware of the ways of the world, comes riding not a mare but a bull, wearing animal skins not silks, decked with ash not sandal paste, serpents not garlands, with ghosts and wild forest spirits instead of family and friends. Parvati's parents are not amused, but Parvati refuses to change her mind. She begs Shiva to temper his form to the satisfaction of her parents, and he, eager to indulge this devotee of his, transforms into the most elegant of beings, Mahadeva, more beautiful than all the devas.

And so Shiva marries Parvati and takes her to Kailas, a mountain peak covered with snow where nothing grows. Here she makes a home even though Shiva does not understand the concept. He is content living in caves during the rains, in crematoriums in winter and on mountain peaks in summer.

Parvati and Shiva make love, but he offers his semen not to her, but the devas. It is so fiery that it burns Agni, the fire-god, and remains resistant to the touch of Vayu, the wind-god. It boils Ganga, the river-goddess, and sets aflame Saravana, the forest of reeds. From the ashes emerge six boys from Shiva's single seed who are nursed by the six star-goddesses who make up the Krittika constellation. Parvati takes the six children in her hand and fuses them into one. Thus is born the six-headed Skanda, warrior-child, who leads the devas into battle and defeats the asuras.

Skanda, or Kartikeya, or Murugan, as he is known in the south, is Shiva's son, born of his seed, incubated in multiple wombs. Parvati now wants a son of her own. Shiva refuses to indulge

Calendar art of Shiva agreeing to marry Parvati

Miniature painting of Shiva's wedding procession

this wish as he says children are needed only by mortal beings who seek rebirth. He is immortal and so has no need for children. Parvati argues that children are also needed to receive and give love.

When Shiva does not grant Parvati what she wants, she anoints her body with turmeric, scrapes it off and from the rubbings creates a child without a man (nayaka), and names him Vinayaka. When Shiva discovers this child, he does not recognise him as Parvati's. In a fit of rage and jealousy, he cuts his head, but when Parvati reveals who the child is, replaces it with an elephant's head to pacify her. Thus is born Ganesha, the god who removes obstacles, associated with affluence and abundance.

The two sons of Shiva, Skanda and Ganesha, take care of the two primal fears of man: fear of being killed by a predator and fear of dying of starvation. Skanda fights the asuras and provides security, while Ganesha removes all obstacles to material prosperity. Thus the sons of the hermit Shiva indulge all the desires of the householder. They would not exist if Parvati had not come into the picture. Parvati thus embodies that aspect of domesticated nature, which evokes the best of the human mind.

Shiva beheads Brahma. Shiva beheads Daksha. Shiva also beheads Vinayaka. With each beheading, a new wisdom emerges. The first marks the destruction of the desire to claim ownership over nature, hence the Goddess. The second marks the destruction of the desire to control culture, hence the Goddess. The third marks the destruction of the desire to block access to nature, hence the Goddess.

Calendar art of Shiva's marriage

Cambodian sculpture of Shiva and Parvati on Nandi

The *Shiva Purana* begins with Shiva's refusal to marry. When married, he is reluctant to make love. When he finally makes loves, he is reluctant to shed semen. When he sheds semen it is not in his wife's womb but outside. He refuses to give Parvati the child she wants. By creating a child on her own, Parvati declares her autonomy. She does not need Shiva. But by then Shiva needs her. He wants to be with her. When Vinayaka blocks his path to her, he removes the obstacle brutally. This violence indicates Shiva, who once loved isolation, now yearns for companionship. Devi thus has successfully domesticated him. She no longer dances on his chest as Kali. She now sits on his lap as Gauri. The hermit (tapasvin) becomes a contributor (yajaman) in the yagna, though he remains a yogi, one who has no desire to be the yagna's beneficiary (bhogi).

Sati exists in the old Vedic way, where yagna was paramount and all that mattered were the rules of exchange that governed the ritual. Sati is destroyed and, when she is reborn, she emerges in a new Puranic order, one where devotion and adoration, expressed trough puja, is preferred. In the yagna-way, there is no clear concept of God; there are only gods or devas. In the puja-way, gods/devas are replaced by God/Mahadeva, the tone is more emotional than technical. Sati rejects Daksha, hence Brahma, but chooses Shiva as husband, and Vishnu as brother, who become focal points of Hindu tradition.

We can say that Sati and Parvati embody the pre-Buddhist and post-Buddhist forms of Hinduism. Pre-Buddhist Vedic Hinduism thrived before 500 BCE. Post-Buddhist Puranic Hinduism thrived after 500 CE. Buddhism, which dominated the subcontinent for nearly a thousand years, was a major transformative force in India, as it questioned the mechanistic and materialistic way

The domestication of Shiva

of the yagna. But the low value given to emotion in Buddhism was addressed by bhakti traditions, which gave rise to temple traditions, stories of the Puranas and the ritual of puja.

The yagna-way valued fire. This fire ultimately consumes Sati. The puja-way values water. Parvati draws out the heat from within Shiva until the ice melts, both metaphorically and literally. She gets Shiva to break the fall of the river Ganga as she descends from the sky and makes its way to earth. In Hindu tradition, the dead are first burned in a funeral pyre and then their ashes are thrown in a river. Fire consumes death but water helps in rebirth. If Sati embraces death, Parvati brings forth life. She rejuvenates and revitalises Shiva, and the world.

Shiva transforms into the dancer Nataraja and the musician Vinapani in the presence of Parvati. She asks him questions on the nature of reality and the world, and their conversations are heard by birds and bulls and fish who transmit this knowledge to the world. The birds transmit the ocean of stories, *Katha-sarit-sagar*. The bull transmits the knowledge of sensory pleasures, Kama-sutra. The fish transforms into Matsyendranath and transmits esoteric knowledge, the Tantras. Thus, with Parvati's presence, the ice melts and water flows in various ways to enrich culture.

Daksha's approach to culture is rather masculine, based on command and control. Parvati's approach is more feminine, based on affection. When Shiva tells Parvati that he does not feel there is any need for a kitchen in Kailas, she disappears. Shortly thereafter the followers of Shiva, the gana, led by Ganapati, go to Shiva and ask him for food. He has none to give. He goes around the world with a begging bowl but finds no food. Finally, he reaches Kashi and finds Parvati's kitchen there. She smiles and says, 'You may

Calendar art of Annapoorna, the kitchen-goddess

Festivals of Gauri in Rajasthan

have outgrown hunger but not others. The kitchen is for them.' As she feeds her children, Shiva declares her to be Annapoorna, goddess of food, the ideal wife for the hermit who has no hunger. While Daksha's masculine gaze is firmly focused on his own needs, Parvati's feminine gaze shifts the focus to others. Culture then becomes an outcome not of domestication but of empathy.

4. Durga's Secret

Everyone lives on the edge in fear

Poster art showing Yoga-maya protecting Krishna

Offerings to Shiva and Vishnu include food, flowers, leaves, lamps and incense. The aim is to invoke God who is otherwise dormant. Offerings to Devi are strikingly different. Besides the standard offerings to God, there is always something more: haldi (turmeric), kunku (red powder), kajal (kohl), and pieces of cloth to serve as her upper garment — the choli (blouse), the chunari (veil) and the chadar (shawl). The aim is to cover up the Goddess so that she is less Kali and more Gauri. Why so?

This makes sense if we associated the male form of divinity with the mind and the female form of divinity with nature. We want to invoke the mind as well as domesticate nature. Only invoking the mind without domesticating nature is the trait of Shiva, the withdrawn hermit. Only domesticating nature without invoking the mind is the trait of Brahma, who manifests as Daksha, the controlling priest. This tension between mind and nature is a key theme of the Puranas.

And so, the preferred form of the Goddess is Durga, riding her lion, defying domestication. Her unbound hair reveals that she is still wild like Kali, but her nose-ring reveals she is domesticated like Gauri. The weapons in her multiple hands reveal a different kind of violence, one that is restrained unlike Kali's, one that offers protection but can also be used to punish. She is Brahma's defiant daughter, Vishnu's protected and protective sister, and Shiva's affectionate wife. Her affection cannot be taken for granted. She will not be exploited. Domestication of the Goddess (nature) must be mirrored with the awakening of God (mind).

Poster art of Kanya-kumari

From the southern tip of India comes a very interesting tale that challenges the very idea of domestication in order to establish culture.

A young girl, Kanya-kumari, meaning one who is a virgin, invokes Shiva and expresses her desire to be his wife. Shiva agrees. But the devas are not pleased with this news. As long as Kanya-kumari is without husband and children, she has the power to kill demons. Her power unused in marriage and motherhood will also prevent the sea from overwhelming the land. So they go out of their way to disrupt this wedding. They tell Kanya-kumari that to ensure the marriage is a happy one she has to marry at sunrise the following day. But Shiva lives far away in the north on Mount Kailas; he must be asked to set forth immediately and travel through the night. Shiva agrees to travel fast, eager to meet his bride, while Kanya-kumari spends the night preparing the wedding feast, adorning herself with cosmetics and jewellery. In the middle of the night, the devas take the form of roosters and start to crow. Shiva thinks the sun is about to rise and that he will not make it to the wedding on time. So he turns around, disappointed. When the sun really does rise, there is no sign of Shiva. A heartbroken Kanya-kumari breaks all the pots containing the wedding feast: the pulses and grains turn into the colourful sand that one finds near the southern tip of India. She washes away her cosmetics in the sea: that is why the sea is multi-coloured there. She stands on the southern tip, killing demons, preventing the sea from overwhelming the land and, like a divine beacon, enabling fishermen to battle tempestuous seas and come home safe to their wives.

This story displays an ambiguous relationship with

Odisha patta painting of the untamed Goddess

domestication. At one level, we want God to be domesticated (he must be a householder, not a hermit), and at another level, we do not want the Goddess to be completely domesticated (she must stay forest, not become field). Typically cultures use rules and laws (niti) and traditional codes of conduct (riti) to stifle freedom for the larger good. But this can destroy creativity and innovation and even introspection. It can amplify our sense of entrapment. So it is important to retain the wildness of nature, which offers the promise of freedom.

This is why in the *Shiva Purana* and in the *Devi Purana,* the devas often prevent Parvati from bearing Shiva's child herself; they would rather that Shiva's seed be germinated in multiple wombs. Parvati, or Gauri, is not mother in the conventional sense of the term. She is foster mother of Kartikeya, and she creates Ganesha using the paste with which she anoints her body. Neither is born through her womb. This may not make literal sense, but it makes a whole lot of symbolic sense.

This rejection of complete domestication is symbolically communicated through the unbound hair of Durga. Traditionally, well-combed and bound hair indicates domestication. But Durga, dressed in bridal finery, sports unbound hair. She thus stands on the edge, between nature and culture, acknowledging our fear of lawless freedom as well as lawful entrapment.

In the last five hundred years, a deliberate attempt has been made in Hinduism to humanise the divine. God is not a lofty concept out there; it is immediate and accessible. And Goddess is not all of nature; she is the village that sustains a human population.

The worship of Durga as the daughter of households in Bengal, Assam and Odisha

These ideas were not new. Grama-devis or village-goddesses are perhaps the oldest form of religion known in India, predating Buddha, even the Vedas, and the Indus valley cities. She was identified with termite hills, and snake holes, and rock clefts, for she emerged from beneath the earth, the seat of all fertility.

But five hundred years ago, the relationship became extremely intimate and personal. It was articulated using a very emotional vocabulary in songs and ritual ceremonies. As God increasingly became parent, child, master, friend, even lover, the Goddess became a member of the family. This came to be known as the bhakti phase of Hinduism, where simple human emotions were made portals to reach the divine. In keeping with this trend, in eastern India, in Bengal, Assam and Odisha, we find the Goddess, who is normally addressed as mother, being treated as the daughter of the village.

Every year, during the autumn months, she returns from her husband's house in the form of Durga for a few days of rest in the comforting arms of her mother, the village community. Thus the mother of the village transforms into the daughter and is indulged accordingly. She comes with her children, two sons, the strong Kartikeya and the smart Ganesha, and her two daughters, the rich Lakshmi and the talented Saraswati. She complains that her husband, Shiva, does not work and she is left to provide for the family. Her mother empathises with her but reminds her that she chose the man she married; no one forced her to marry a hermit who wanders with dogs and ghosts, lives in crematoriums, and loves narcotics. She is bathed, and clothed, and fed, and entertained with songs and dances. And finally, she is bid farewell, cast into the river, where her image dissolves, as she makes her way back to

Images of Subhadra with her brothers in Puri, Odisha

her husband's house in faraway snow-capped Mount Kailas.

This happens year after year. She comes and she goes. They weep in joy on her arrival and weep in sorrow at her departure. Thus the cyclical nature of the world is reinforced to the village community. Nothing lasts forever. Nothing ends forever. Everything comes back. Everything goes back. It grants solace and hope to the villagers who are facing sorrow. It also warns those who are enjoying fortune not to take things for granted.

What strikes the eye when one closely observes the traditional image of Durga in Bengal is her turmeric yellow skin. She is therefore called Haldi-mukhi, she of the turmeric face. Haldi, or turmeric, is an essential feature of Goddess-worship. It is both an antiseptic and a cosmetic that keeps the skin clean and makes it glow like gold.

In the temple of Krishna in Puri, Odisha, there is another Haldi-mukhi, the goddess Subhadra, Krishna's sister, standing between him and his elder brother Balabhadra. The similar complexion of Durga and Subhadra reminds us of temple lore that Devi who is Shiva's wife is also Vishnu's sister.

In his various avatars, Vishnu keeps fighting for his sister. In one of the folk Mahabharatas is the story of a warrior who saw the entire war at Kurukshetra from the top of a mountain; he had been decapitated before the war but Krishna had kept his head alive so that his last wish of witnessing the war could be fulfilled. When asked what he saw, he declared he only saw Krishna's discus cutting the head of unrighteous kings, and Kali drinking their blood by spreading her tongue over the battlefield.

Miniature painting of the birth of Durga

Simultaneously, this sister protected the world from Madhu and Kaitabha when Vishnu was in a dreamless slumber. It was she who offered herself as sacrifice to save baby Krishna from the murderous Kansa. It was she who ensured Shiva no longer shuts his eyes to the world, that he fathered Kartikeya and Ganesha who protect and provide culture. And when an asura emerges, whom neither Indra, nor Vishnu, nor Shiva can defeat, it is she who is once again invoked.

Thus in the *Devi Mahatmya,* when Indra begs Brahma for help and Brahma takes him to Vishnu and Vishnu takes him to Shiva, Shiva advises all the devas to release the Goddess from within their bodies and merge it to create a Goddess who is greater than all of them individually. Flames emerge from the body of each and every deva and these flames merge in a blinding light to create Durga, who is given weapons by each deva, and who then rides a lion to do battle with an asura. Durga thus is the jigsaw puzzle whose parts come from the different devas. They are 'parts' and she is the 'whole'. She is not the daughter of one deva, she is the daughter of all devas; she is ayonija, born without a womb, with no mother of her own. This establishes her as Mahadevi, the goddess of the gods, just as Shiva is Mahadeva, god of the gods. Thus the Puranas acknowledge her sovereignty. She is, like Shiva and Vishnu, swayambhu or self-created.

Who is this asura that Durga has to defeat? Who is this 'demon' who overpowers god (deva) and God (Mahadeva)? He is identified as Mahisha-asura, the buffalo demon, though he takes many forms, that of an elephant, lion and even human, and fights with

Miniature painting of Durga killing Mahisha-asura

numerous types of weapons, before he is finally killed.

Those who prefer to see mythology as proto-history see this as a story that retells the epic conquest of fair-skinned, cow-loving Aryans of the north over dark-skinned, buffalo-loving Dravidians of the south. The problem with this reading is that here the warrior is a woman and it is hard for scholars to reconcile Vedic patriarchy with the obvious female power embedded in the Durga image. Besides, many scholars have long debunked this racial theory popular in the early 20th century.

Those who see mythology as proto-psychology conclude that Durga destroys the slippery, shape-shifting human ego that seeks dominion over nature. But what is ego?

This word comes to us from Freudian and Jungian psychoanalysis of the 20th century. The word used in Upanishads composed 2,500 years ago is aham. We have assumed they mean the same thing. But do they really?

Aham means how humans imagine themselves as against atma, who we really are. Animals do not have any doubt about who they are in terms of location in the food chain and pecking order. All they care about when they see another animal is: is that a predator, a prey, a rival or a mate? Humans are confused. There is no such clear understanding. Imagination wipes out all structures and we are forced into a struggle between our own desires (how we want to imagine ourselves) and social structures imposed upon us by others based on their desires (how others are expected to see us). More often than not we regress to our animal selves: we want to dominate or be dominated, we want to domesticate others with rules or be domesticated by them. This is Mahisha, the asura. A deva then is one who recognises, like Indra, that there are larger

Poster images of Durga

forces at work in the universe, embodied in Brahma, Vishnu, Shiva and of course, Devi. Mahisha acknowledges Brahma but seeks to triumph over others, and in doing so lies his folly. Mahisha-asura's defeat is not viewed as submission but as realisation: he breaks free from his limited self-indulgent view of the world and internalises the bigger picture. This is called uddhar, or upliftment.

But these are lofty ideas. How were these communicated to simple folk who lived in villages? Our question is presumptuous. We assume that great knowledge cannot come from 'simple rural folk'. We assume that wise brahmins came up with these ideas and passed them on. But the more one studies Indian rituals and texts, the more one realises that the wisdom of India comes from 'simple rural folk', simply articulated in Sanskrit. The brahmins are scribes, compilers and organisers, not sources, of Vedic wisdom. This becomes evident when we look at village rituals associated with the worship of grama-devi. Today, these practices are seen more in the southern part of India, but there are traces in the north too. They are usually seen in technologically backward rural communities who communicate deep psychological ideas through symbols and rituals, rather than words.

Unlike Durga, who is associated with the entire universe, the grama-devi is restricted to her neighbourhood. She makes the universal particular. She embodies the settlement: she is Mumba-devi of Mumbai, Chandika of Chandigarh, Kali of Kolkata. Her image is often just a rock that marks either the navel of the village, or the periphery. Eyes are painted on the rock to indicate she is sensitive to the condition of villagers. She is shown wearing a nose-

Photograph of Saptashrungi-devi of Maharashtra

Photograph of Mhasoba in Pune, Maharashtra

ring, indicator of her domestication. Her palms are either raised to indicate she offers protection, or lowered to indicate she offers bounty. Rarely does she have a body: the village is her body. She is sometimes accompanied by a twin-goddess, identified as her sister or as her friend or just a companion who takes care of her devotees when she wants to rest. Her attendants are brave men, the viras, often with moustaches to emphasise their masculinity, and riding horses in the company of hunting dogs. In south India, the vira is often a Muslim cavalry officer indicating close association with village realities. He is the guardian god who forms a complementary pair with the fertility goddess. He protects; she provides.

Three things are striking in the worship of grama-devi. First, the practice of actually sacrificing a buffalo, or a male goat, or even a rooster, to the Goddess, and mixing her blood with rice and throwing this into fields where crops have just been harvested. Second, the practice of keeping images of Mhasoba (the buffalo-lord), or Pothraj (the buffalo-king) alongside Durga, describing him as her attendant, and sometimes even her husband, who is then called Bhairava, a form of Shiva. There is at least one Puranic tale where Durga finds a Shiva-linga in the throat of the asura. Third, the practice of mostly male devotees ritually torturing themselves for her pleasure during her festival. They swing from hooks, pierce their tongue, walk on fire, whip and even bite themselves. In some parts of the Deccan, in Maharashtra, Karnataka and Andhra Pradesh, the priest who serves the Goddess is called Pothraj, and he typically belongs to non-brahmin communities. At times, the priests dress as women and carry the sacred pot on their head. All this reveals an ambiguous relationship between Durga and the buffalo. Is it only demon or also a god? A villain or also a hero? An

Photograph of Vaishno-devi of Jammu

Photograph of Bhairava

abuser or also a husband? Does the buffalo represent the 'aham' of devotees?

While in most stories Bhairava comes to the rescue of the goddess, in the story of Vaishno-devi, Bhairava is her abuser. Vaishno-devi's temple is located to the north, in Jammu. Unlike other goddesses, she does not demand blood (this is fairly common of grama-devis of the Jammu and Himachal areas). The story goes that she was Vedavati who resisted the charms and attentions of many men as she was determined to marry Vishnu. When Bhairava tried to force himself on her, she ran through the hills, hid in caves, and finally transformed into the fiery goddess who beheaded Bhairava and then forgave him, after he apologised for his presumptuousness. So, today, those who visit the shrine of Vaishno-devi also visit the shrine of Bhairava. Once her abuser, he is now her guardian. The violence of the tale re-links us with the tale of Shiva beheading Brahma. Ultimately, for culture to happen, domestication has to be voluntary, born of love, not the desire to control.

In one of the many stories associated with Bahuchara-mata in Gujarat, a young bride on her way to her husband's house kills herself to save herself from being assaulted by a highway robber. She curses the highway robber that he will only attain liberation from worldly bondage if he castrates himself and serves as her eunuch-priestess. In another story, a young bride discovers that her husband — who never comes to her room at night, instead riding out on his horse — is (depending on various versions of this oral tale) a homosexual, or a transgendered person, or a cross-dresser, locally known as hijra. Furious that he tricked her into a false marriage that will ruin her life, she turns into a goddess, punishes her husband, and offers him salvation from worldly

Poster art of Bahuchara-mata of Gujarat

bondage only if he becomes a hijra and serves her. Members of the hijra community castrate themselves taking her name. Her temple is also popular with women seeking children. Here too we find the tension associated with marriage, fertility, and woman's frustration in marriage. Here, the demon is husband and abuser.

At the heart of the ambiguous relationship of the grama-devi with her male attendants is humanity's relationship with nature. Humans establish culture by domesticating nature. The process of domestication is a violent one: rivers are blocked, forests are burned, and mountains are razed. In mythological terms, the mother is violated to create the daughter. And she strikes back in various ways, demanding appeasement. She will not be taken for granted. The buffalo-demon then is humanity seeking to control nature, who is at once father, brother and son. He needs to be punished when he crosses the line. But he is also venerated, as he has divinity within him which can be evoked. What is the divinity within man? What is the God who can be awakened? It is the ability to empathise with the world around, with nature and with fellow humans, that keeps human cupidity and stupidity in check.

The grama-devi embodies not just the village but also each and every woman in the village. In many ways, she is the goddess. Her house is the temple. And she is her own priestess. Traditionally, it is she who plastered the house and floor with cow dung each day and painted images on and in front of it with rice flour. This ritual painting is called kolam in Tamil Nadu, rangoli in Maharashtra and alpana in Bengal. She invoked the goddess through rituals known as vrata, which did not involve the intervention of priests. It

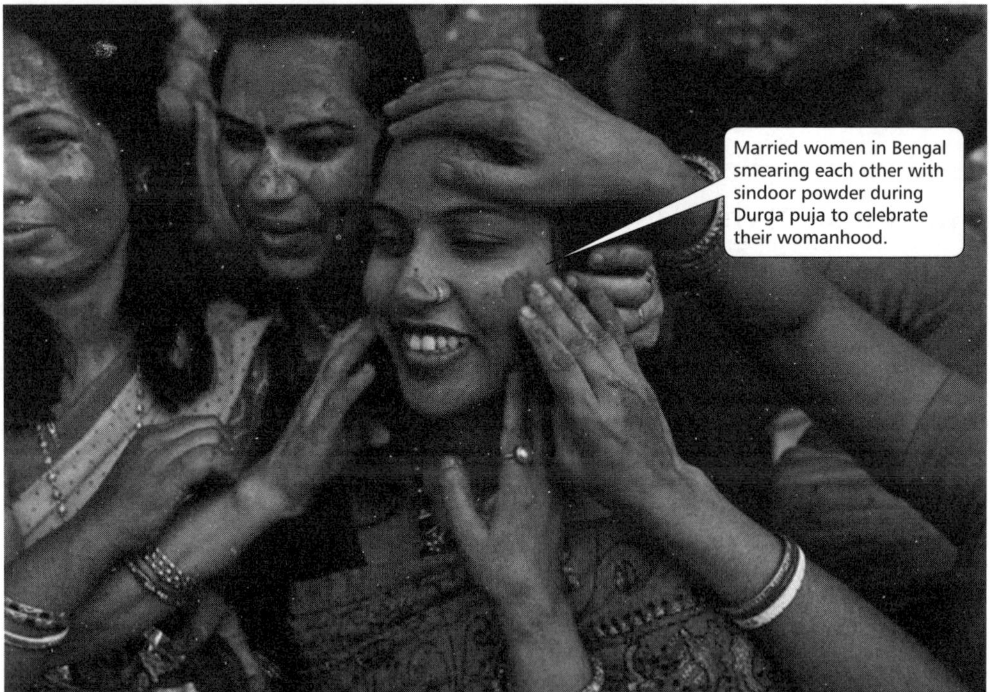

Women's rituals

involved her either staying away from a particular form of food or eating a particular form of food. Her rituals brought in good energy into the household, ensured prosperity and peace. Her anger and unhappiness brought in disease. She was the diminutive double of the goddess, dressed as such during the wedding ceremony. Her entry into the house was celebrated as if a goddess were entering the house. For with her entry, the kitchen fire would survive for yet another generation and she would bring forth the next generation of the clan.

In south and west India especially, women hold ceremonies called 'haldi-kunku', during which married women gather and greet each other with turmeric, red powder, flowers and gifts. This is a ritual of women, for women. Widows are not allowed, reaffirming the ritual's links with fertility more than femininity. A similar festival is found in Bengal, where married women smear each other with vermilion powder on the final day of Durga puja.

Domestication of women mirrored domestication of nature. Her freedom was curtailed as she approached puberty. She was not allowed to cook or touch anyone when she was menstruating. She was valued for being fertile and feared when she was not fertile, as during menstruation, or after she became a widow. This created anxiety, depression and frustration in women, which was the common explanation given for 'hysterical trances', a way of letting out repressed emotions. Traditionally this was explained with the phrase 'the devi has come', making women the medium of the goddess who spoke what otherwise could never be spoken.

Stories of goddesses in rural shrines often reflect this tension

Poster art showing Renuka-Yellamma and her story

between the village and nature, as well as the tension between women and men in marriage. The most popular of these stories is that of Renuka-Yellamma. There is a scriptural Sanskrit version of this story in the Puranas, as well as an oral version of the story.

In the Puranic version, Renuka one day sees a handsome gandharva bathing in a river. For a moment she harbours sexual desire for him. Until then she has thought of no one else sexually except her husband, Jamadagni, a great tapasvin. The sage senses her momentary lack of fidelity and demands that she be beheaded. The sons who refuse to do so are cursed to turn into eunuchs. The youngest son, Parashuram, raises his axe and severs his mother's neck.

There are many oral versions of what happens next. In one version, when the father offers his obedient son a boon, Parashuram asks his mother be brought back to life, and she is, thanks to Jamadagni's powers accumulated through tapasya. In another version, a non-brahmin woman tries to stop the matricide and gets decapitated herself; Parashuram replaces his mother's head on the non-brahmin woman's body and the non-brahmin head on his mother's body, creating confusion as to who is his real mother. In still another version, the head and body become deities in their own rights: the head is Yellamma and the body is Huligamma. Here, the tension is not just about fidelity, it is also about caste.

In the oral version of the Renuka-Yellamma story, a young brahmin girl discovers that her husband is no brahmin and in fury beheads him. Some believe this story belongs to a distinctively different grama-devi, often addressed as Ammaveru, whose name means 'the lady', a generic title for the village-goddess.

Photograph of a devadasi of Yellamma

While in the Puranic story it is the woman who is killed, in the folk story it is the man who is killed. In the Puranic story, the brahmin woman is killed because she is 'contaminated' by her adulterous desire as well as by her contact with the non-brahmin woman. In the oral story, the man who is killed is a brahmin-pretender.

Both the body and the head of Renuka are objects of worship, especially in the Deccan region of India. Known variously as Yellamma or Huligamma, she is invoked by women for children, and is commonly associated with the devadasi cult, women who were not bound by limitations of marriage. While this was meant to give these women freedom to choose lovers without losing social standing, it often ended up making them prostitutes as they were denied all sources of wealth.

Chaste women are described in scriptures as Sati and associated with magical powers. Renuka, for example, before she desired another man, had the power to collect water in unbaked pots. In the Ramayana, Sita is able to walk through fire because she is chaste in mind and body. In the Puranas, there is the story of Shilavati, who is able to stop even the sun from rising using the power of chastity. Chastity even makes a wife more powerful than the gods, as we learn from the story of Anasuya.

On the request of their wives, Shiva, Vishnu and Brahma take the form of three young men trying to seduce Anasuya, the chaste wife of Atri. They ask that she let them suckle her breasts so that they can end their vow of fasting. Anasuya agrees, but such is the power of her chastity that no sooner does she bare her breasts than the gods turn into children, and are restored to their normal form

Poster art of Anasuya

only when the wives of the gods apologise.

The belief was that a sati protected her husband with the powers of chastity. When Vrinda's husband, an asura called Jalandhar, was killed by devas, everyone accused her of infidelity. She then learned that Vishnu himself had come to her house taking the form of Jalandhar. A Vishnu devotee, she was furious that he had tricked her so, and she demanded justice. Vishnu was cursed into the shaligrama stone for his overzealous determination to save the devas, while Vrinda was transformed into the tulsi plant and kept in the courtyard of the house – outside yet inside. No worship of Vishnu is complete without offerings of tulsi sprigs. She is present in everyone's house to remind women of the power of chastity.

Belief that a woman's chastity protects her husband led to the popularisation of the infamous 'sati' practices, especially amongst warrior communities like the Rajputs, where women burned themselves on the funeral pyre of their husbands killed in war. This practice was valorised and glamorised, with these women turned into goddesses. It was expected to be voluntary, with everyone believing that the power of Sati would protect these women from the heat of the flames. Rani-sati-mata is still worshipped in Rajasthan and many parts of India, though the practice has been made illegal as this belief has been seen as enabling the oppression and mistreatment of women.

Sita and Draupadi, the female protagonists of the two great epics of Hinduism, the Ramayana and the Mahabharata, are always on the edge between the wild and sovereign Kali and the demure and dependent Gauri. They appear as wives but, when challenged, display their Kali-like form. They are not forced to domesticate

Worship of epic heroines

themselves; they choose to domesticate themselves out of empathy for humanity. Any attempt to force them to be domestic, as Renuka is, transforms them into fiery goddesses who refuse to be tamed. This is reinforced in the story of Sita who has many reasons to be unfaithful to her husband Ram, who continuously doubts her chastity, but she refuses to turn her back on him.

But Draupadi refuses to take her abuse lying down and demands blood. In the Mahabharata, the Kauravas try to publicly disrobe Draupadi, declaring her a public woman as she has five husbands. A furious Draupadi displays her rage by refusing to tie her hair until she has washed it with the blood of her abusers. She stops being the demure Gauri and evokes Kali. This so frightens the father of the Kauravas that he begs Draupadi to leave the gambling hall with her dignity intact, along with her husbands who had foolishly gambled themselves and her away. Eventually, the war happens, and Draupadi washes her hair with the blood of her abusers. So in south India, Draupadi is worshipped just like other grama-devis as Amman, the mother, who is terrifying and needs appeasement. Amongst grama-devis, Draupadi is much more popular than the silent, stoic Sita, sadly projected as a whimpering, heartbroken doormat even in 20th-century feminist retellings.

In the Mahabharata is the story of the wives of the seven celestial sages who encounter Agni, the fire-god. Six of the seven women approach him without wearing symbols of marriage. As a result, the heat and light of the fire-god makes them pregnant. In later versions, they enter a pond in which Shiva is meditating and so get

Images of disease goddesses

pregnant because of Shiva's power that percolates into the water. Their husbands accuse them of infidelity and cast them out of the house. They abort the foetuses in their bodies and go into the forest. The aborted foetuses set the forest afire. When the flames die out, the six foetuses merge into a single child – the warlord Skanda also known as Murugan. The women try to attack him, but he calms them down by acknowledging them as his mothers, and declares that whosoever fails to respect them will suffer. They will have the power to cause miscarriages and kill children with measles, pox and cholera.

Thus, outside the village, often associated with the grama-devi herself, are shrines of goddesses associated with disease and death. They are called Jari-Mari, she who makes the body hot and feverish, or Shitala, she who makes the body cool. From time to time she is offered neem leaves, lemons, and sour curds, along with wedding finery, to make her happy so that she leaves the women and children of the village alone.

The worship of Shitala is an interesting facet of Hinduism. In most cultures, the undesirable is wiped out. But in Hinduism, the undesirable is also considered valid and given due dignity. She who causes fever, pox and skin rashes is worshipped as a goddess: she is considered a part of nature, an undesirable part of nature, but nature nevertheless. She is acknowledged but respectfully asked to stay away from the household. Everyone knows the consequences of ignoring her. She will strike with vengeance, defying every fence and every rule created by man, wiping out all that culture seeks to establish.

The ferocity of this aspect of Devi is evident in the story of Periyachi Amman, found in Tamil Nadu, and even in Singapore

Periyachi, the midwife goddess

and Malaysia where the worship of the Goddess has travelled. There was once a rather nasty king who troubled his subjects. When his wife conceived a child, the oracles foretold that if the child's feet ever touched the ground the world would come to an end. So when the queen went into labour, not a single midwife was willing to offer her services. Finally the Goddess came out of pity for the suffering woman. As soon as the child was delivered, the Goddess held the child in her arms, not wanting to put it on the ground, and asked the king for her payment. He refused to pay knowing that the midwife could do nothing – if she placed the child on the ground, the earth would be destroyed and she would die too. The Goddess was amused. She sprouted several pairs of hands. She ripped open the queen's belly. She crushed the king underfoot. But all the while she kept the child in her hand above the ground to ensure the world did not come to an end.

This story shows the two sides of the Goddess, the malevolent one as well as the benevolent one. Nature can be cruel and kind. We may try to domesticate her in our favour but we have to be wary of her other, darker, side.

The words Durga and Shakti are often used synonymously. But there is a subtle difference. Shakti means power that is natural. Durga evokes 'durg', or the fortress that is artificial. Thus Shakti embodies energy that is natural, while Durga embodies power that is cultural. In culture, power is created through laws. These laws shift power from the strong to provide security to the weak. This makes Durga the defender of the weak, to be invoked at wartime by warriors and kings. She is the protector of the fort,

Poster art of Durga appearing before Ram

the patron of kings, and rides into battle on a lion, dressed as a bride, but with unbound hair, her multiple arms bearing a variety of lethal weapons.

In the Ramayana, Ravana and Ram invoke Durga; in Bengali lore, Ram offers her one of his eyes to replace a missing lotus. In the Mahabharata, the Kauravas and Pandavas invoke Durga; in Tamil lore, Arjun sacrifices his son, Aravan. Those who sacrifice end up winners. What do they sacrifice? Ram's eye and Arjun's son embody attachment. Attachment is sacrificed. Attachment to what? Attachment to our delusions, what we assume to be the truth.

In the jungle, there are no heroes, villains or victims. But in culture, there are heroes, villains and victims. We feel we are victimised and seek heroes who will destroy villains. This is humanity's greatest delusion.

One day, a king saw a hawk chase a dove. He decided to save the dove from being killed. 'What will I eat now?' asked the hawk. When the king asked him to eat something else, he said, 'Why should someone else die so that you can save the dove?' When the king asked him to eat something vegetarian, he replied: 'Nature made me a carnivore. Do you think you can improve on nature?'

Human imagination enables us to judge nature and rejects its ways. We reject the way of the jungle, which favours only the fit. We create society where rules ensure even the unfit can survive. By doing so we create victims, villains and heroes. The rules are supposed to save those victimised by nature (the unfit). Those who uphold the law are heroes and those who break it are the villains.

But different communities subscribe to different sets of laws.

Posters depicting complementary aspects of the Goddess

Which is the correct law? Which law works for all? Laws that favour tribal communities (protect the forest) work against laws that favour agricultural communities (create more fields). Laws which favour agricultural communities do not favour urban communities (buildings and office and industrial complexes). What is fair for one is not fair for another (laws that favour heterosexuals and exclude homosexuals). This leads to conflict, war, in which Durga is invoked. More laws, fairer and just laws, are established but they remain laws nevertheless.

In the forest, no animals complain. They accept their place in the food chain and pecking order. They know that nothing is permanent. A predator in one context (snake chasing rat) is a prey in another context (hawk chasing snake). A dominant alpha must give way to a younger, stronger alpha, who invariably emerges eventually. Humans seek rules that establish a permanent world – hence the quest for the elixir of immortality (amrita) in the Puranas which creates Amravati of the devas. But Amravati of the devas is constantly under siege, threatened by asuras who seek to overrun it. The devas fight, seek the help of Shiva, Vishnu and Durga, but forget Shakti, the inner strength, that enables us to appreciate that notions of fairness and justice are human constructs, that different people have different notions of what is fair and just, and hence the conflict.

Inner strength enables us to see that from the point of others, we may be the villains. We are the asuras who are troubling the devas; we are not necessarily the devas who need Durga's help. It is we who have to be beheaded. Our aham is the root cause of the

Goddess of kings

problems around us. Confronting the truth about us is not easy. It needs Shakti. We need to acknowledge that all problems come from fears, our own fears and the fears of those around us. Once we do that, we will be able to evoke the Durga in us, who comforts, protects and empowers the frightened.

5. Lakshmi's Secret

Wealth can liberate

Popular image of eight forms of Lakshmi, all seated on a lotus

The living (sajiva, in Sanskrit) seek food, the lifeless (ajiva) and the dead (nirjiva) don't. This makes food the fundamental target (laksh) of life. From laksh comes Lakshmi. Lakshmi is food (anna) in nature and wealth (dhana) in culture.

Lakshmi is called Kamala, or lotus. Just as the fragrance, colour and nectar of the lotus attracts bees, food attracts all living creatures. Plants go towards sunlight; animals towards pasture and prey. Food never goes to anyone; everyone comes to food.

The quest for Lakshmi establishes the food chain: plants seek sunlight and water for nourishment, herbivorus animals seek plants for nourishment, and carnivorus animals seek other animals for nourishment.

The quest for Lakshmi also creates the pecking order. Herbivores form groups called herds to secure themselves. Carnivores form groups called packs to improve their chances of finding prey. Within the herd and the pack, there is hierarchy based on strength. The strongest is the alpha, who dominates, and gets access to most food and more mates. The omega is the weakest, gets the least amount of food and the fewest mates. Thus the hierarchy ensures only the fittest survive so that the next generation is fitter than the previous one, hence more likely to survive.

The lion is the alpha carnivore, on top of the food chain. But even the lion does not attack the elephant, which is much bigger. The elephant has no natural predator, and unlike the lion, it feeds every day. That is why the elephant is most closely associated with Lakshmi.

Another reason why Lakshmi is closely associated with the

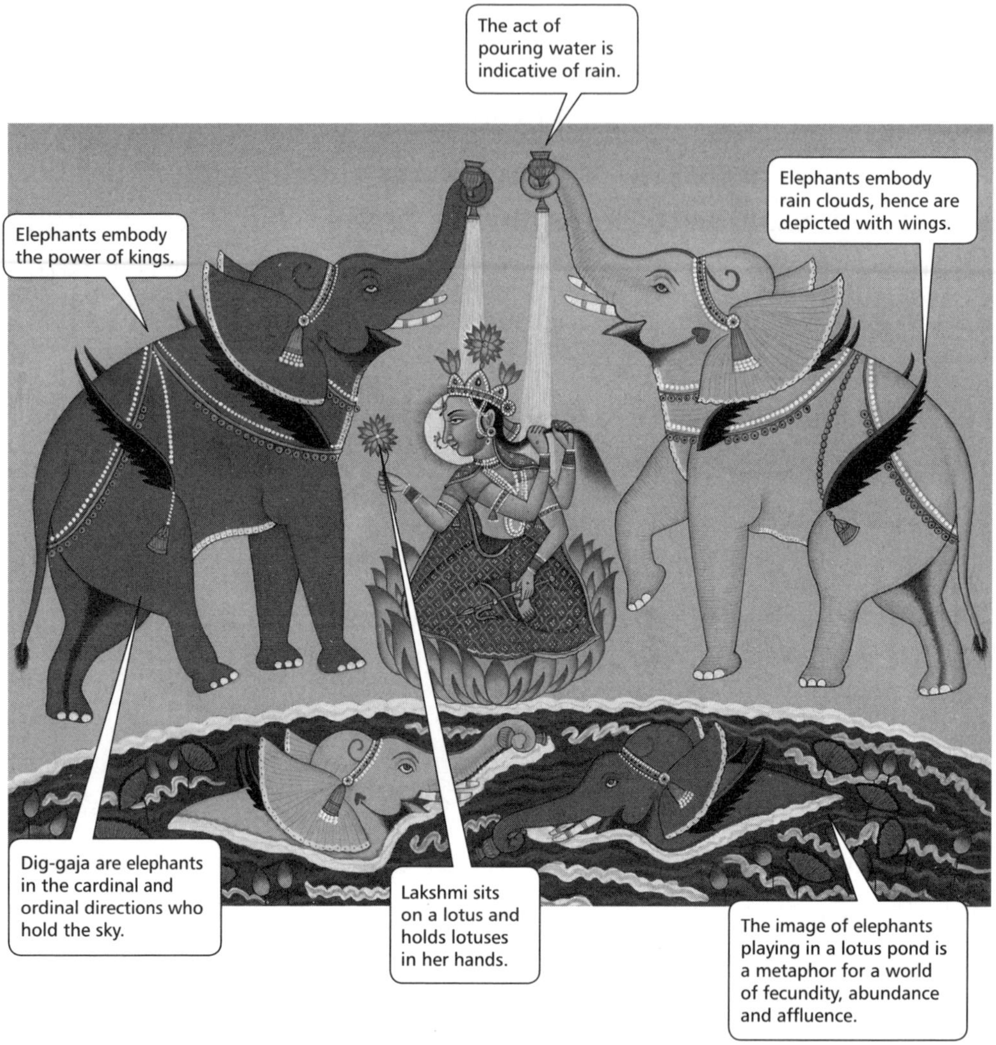

Miniature painting showing Lakshmi with elephants

elephant is because the animal is always associated with water. Where there is water there is life; where there is lots of water, there are usually elephants. Elephants love swimming and they spray water on each other using their trunks. A pair of elephants are often shown spraying Lakshmi with water using their upraised trunks, evoking rain. Dark thunderous monsoon clouds are equated with a herd of trumpeting elephants. In drought, the one animal that always knows where there is water is the old matriarch of the herd who has lived longer than any other animal in the forest.

The Puranas state that there are eight pairs of elephants located at the cardinal and ordinal directions. These are the dig-gajas that hold up the sky in some texts and the earth in others. These are not ordinary elephants; they are special, white as cow's milk, for cow's milk was the much-cherished wealth of the Vedic people who chanted the Shri Sukhta hymn in praise of Lakshmi three thousand years ago.

In the Puranas, Lakshmi has three fathers: Varuna, Puloman and Bhrigu. Varuna is asura in the Vedas, but in the Puranas he becomes a deva, a god of the sea, source of all water. The Puranas describe Puloman as the asura-king and Bhrigu as the asura-guru. This makes Lakshmi the daughter of asuras.

The word 'asura' has been given a moral turn in recent times; they are visualised in children's books as dark-skinned and fat and ugly with horns, the embodiment of evil. It is easy then to assume that Lakshmi's association with asuras stems from the fear of materialism and the corrupting influence of wealth. But equating asuras with evil, and by extension devas with good, is

Images of Digga-pala, guardians of the directions, who are closely linked to Lakshmi more a convenient translation than a correct one, the result of a Judeo-Christian-Islamic lens that came to India first via Mughal rulers and then via British rulers.

In the Puranas, devas and asuras are both children of Brahma. Devas live in the sky and asuras below the earth. All wealth exists below the earth, for it is below the earth that seeds sprout, metal is created and water is hidden. To pull this wealth out, we need the sun (Surya), the wind (Vayu), fire (Agni) and rain (Indra); in other words, we need devas, who then become 'gods', as their actions favour humanity. Asuras become 'demons' as they resist sharing Lakshmi with humanity.

Varuna, as god of the sea, gives its wealth of salt and fish and pearls freely, without asking anything in return. That is why perhaps Varuna is not asura, but deva. Varuna is also the symbol of generosity: one is who is truly affluent.

Puloman rules the land below the earth and does not release Lakshmi easily. Humanity has to invent complex agricultural and mining processes to procure wealth from the earth. The wealth obtained is called Pulomi, which means daughter of Puloman, another name for Lakshmi.

Bhrigu, guru of the asuras, is associated with prediction and foresight. His son Shukra is associated with creativity. A man who can predict the future, who has foresight and is creative, is more likely to create wealth. That is why Lakshmi is called Bhargavi, daughter of Bhrigu. That makes her Shukra's sister.

Lakshmi's value comes only when she leaves her father's realm, when she is no longer immersed in water or buried under the earth. The creation of wealth then is a violent process: forests have to be destroyed to make way for fields and human

Poster art showing Lakshmi with Vishnu

settlements. Raw materials have to be pulled out of the ground for industries. In other words, 'asuras' have to be killed to obtain Lakshmi. She dazzles only when she leaves her father's realm and is seen seated beside Indra, god of the sky, bringer of rain, lord of Amravati.

Wealth that belongs to humans, which has been acquired from nature, is best represented by the pot. The pot is a human invention that allows people to own water and carry it wherever they go. It is the symbol of cultural intervention, of industry and market, creating value out of natural resources. Water in the forest is available for all animals; but water in a pot belongs to the owner of the pot and whosoever he or she gives it to. The pot that is Lakshmi belongs to Indra, and has been wrenched away from the asuras.

The asuras who are killed by devas are time and again resurrected by Shukra, who has the secret known as Sanjivani-vidya, which brings the dead back to life. This alludes to the fertility of the earth which brings back crops year after year. The act of harvesting the crops is equated with the killing of the asuras by devas, an act of violence that enables Lakshmi to come into the house of the farmer. Thus harvest festivals of India, be it vasant-navaratri (Goddess worship in spring) or sharad-navaratri (Goddess worship in autumn), marking the winter and summer agricultural cycles of India, are invariably associated with the killing of asuras: for example, Durga kills Mahisha-asura in Dassera and Krishna kills Naraka-asura in Diwali. That is why the battle between devas and asuras is cyclical. It will never end as long as humans depend on harvesting nature's bounty and seek the regeneration of nature's fertility.

Miniature painting of Indra, king of the gods

As Indra's wife, Lakshmi is known as Sachi and Indra is known as Sachin. The arrival of Lakshmi turns Amravati into Swarga, or paradise. For she brings with her Kalpataru, the wish-fulfilling tree; Kama-dhenu, the wish-fulfilling cow; Chinta-mani, the wish-fulfilling jewel; the Akshaya-patra, the cornucopia, the pot that is always overflowing with grain and gold. These treasures enable the devas to live a life of luxury. They do not have to work a single day. They simply have to make a wish and their desires come true. It is an enviable lifestyle.

What is never clarified in the Puranas is why Indra is entitled to all the pleasures that Lakshmi has to offer. It is simply assumed that wealth belongs to the devas. No explanation is offered.

Modern retellings often equate asuras with the 'original' forest-dwellers who were displaced by deva 'migrants' who came with superior agricultural and pastoral technology. This is how the eternal battle between asuras and devas is explained sociologically. Marxist anthropologists equate devas as the 'haves' and the asuras as the 'have-nots'. Traditionalists tend to describe devas as 'good' and thus entitled to Lakshmi, but this does not make any sense as Indra in the Puranas is always shown drunk with soma-rasa, immersed in sensory pleasures offered by apsaras, often being indifferent, even rude, to sages.

From the asura point of view, Indra is a thief. But unless the devas 'steal' Lakshmi out of the subterranean realm, Lakshmi cannot have value. The asuras do not see it this way. They simply want their daughter/sister back. So they lay siege to Amravati and constantly fight the devas. This turns paradise into an eternal battleground, or rana-bhoomi, with devas constantly struggling to hold on to their wealth. Indra thus has prosperity but no peace.

Miniature painting of Krishna with Satyabhama

This naturally makes asuras, source of Indra's great displeasure, the villains of the Puranas.

We can equate Indra and the devas with 'wealth-generators' and 'value-creators' who are often at the receiving end of criticism because the process of generating wealth is invariably violent: ecosystems are destroyed and people are compelled to do work so that industries and markets can thrive.

Wealth generation also creates social divides on economic lines, for those who establish industries and markets (devas?) feel entitled to claim the lion's share of the wealth generated, much more than those who actually work in industries and markets (asuras?) who end up feeling deprived and often exploited.

The devas can also be inheritors who have not earned anything but have the benefit of enjoying vast wealth because they were born in a particular family. Indra is unable to see the unfairness of the situation because he is born into privilege. He is unable to see the rage of the asuras. Each one demonises the other. Neither understands the other.

The conflict between devas and asuras is very much like the conflict between capitalists and socialists. For the devas, the battle is between those who create wealth and those who do not create wealth. For the asuras, the battle is between those who steal wealth and those who do not steal wealth. What is 'wealth-creation' for one group is 'wealth-theft' for another group. Neither can agree about who should get the lion's share of the wealth generated. Each one is therefore convinced the other is wrong, resulting in a relentless 'righteous' battle.

Shri on a Buddhist stupa

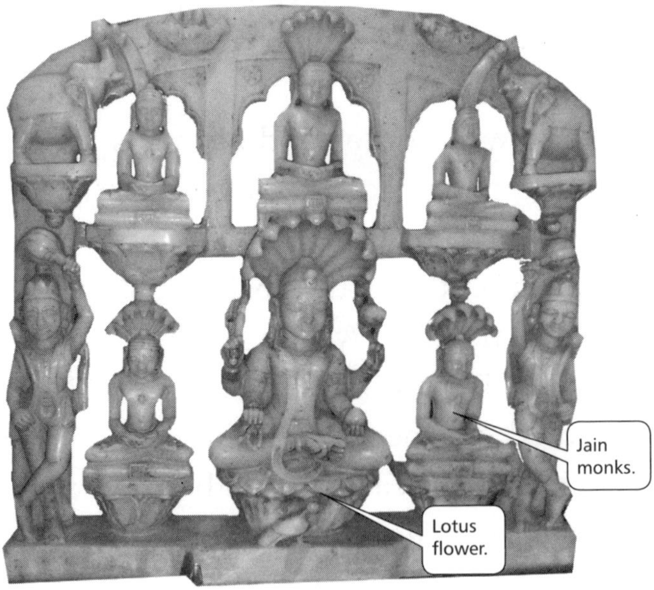

Padmavati (yakshi) surrounded by Jain sages

As Shri, Lakshmi is part of Buddhist and Jain mythology. Her image is found on Buddhist stupas. She is even worshipped as the guardian goddess Padmavati in Jain temples. She is described as wife of Sakra, or Indra. In that role, she is more commonly addressed as Sachi. But while Indra may be happy with Lakshmi by his side, Lakshmi never seems happy to be beside Indra. She seems restless, always on the lookout for someone worthier.

Lakshmi is sometimes visualised seated next to Kubera, the rich king of the yakshas, who hoards treasure. Kubera is identified as Indra's treasurer in some texts, but other texts identify Kubera's wife as Nidhi, goddess of treasures, another name for Lakshmi.

Sachi is often described as being more faithful to Indra's throne than to Indra the person, for Indra can be easily replaced by one more worthy. This is why Indra is always insecure, never able to enjoy his vast wealth. His throne is always shaky, threatened by rishis, rajas and asuras. That is why Lakshmi is called chanchala or whimsical, even cock-eyed (Lokhi-tera, in Bengali). No one is ever sure who the goddess of wealth and fortune will favour. She can appear suddenly without reason, and leave without warning.

Indra gets nervous when a rishi performs tapasya and seeks to generate tapa, the mental fire that will grant siddhi, powers that will enable the rishi to control devas. So he sends apsaras to seduce the rishis and disrupt their tapasya. He steals horses and disrupts yagnas of rajas so that they are not a threat to his power. And he constantly runs to his father Brahma seeking help to kill asuras who lay siege to his paradise. He knows that he is king because of Lakshmi, and his kingdom is Swarga because of Lakshmi. This narrative reflects the insecurity that comes with wealth. The rich

Poster art showing Ravana abducting Sita

Poster art showing Draupadi being gambled away

are never secure about their possessions; they constantly feel that people around them wish to steal what is theirs. This state of mind is the rana-bhoomi, the eternal battle that consumes Indra's paradise.

The story goes that once Lakshmi left Indra's side and went to the asura-king Prahalad. Brahma advised Indra to disguise himself as a servant and serve Prahalad diligently to find out why Lakshmi favoured him over Indra. Indra did as advised and Prahalad finally revealed his secret, 'Lakshmi is attracted to men of actions that demonstrate strength and smartness. If you display strength and shrewdness, she will come to you. If fail to do that, she will not stay with you for long.' Later, when Prahalad offered the disguised Indra a boon, Indra very shrewdly asked for all the merits that Prahalad had obtained through his strong and shrewd actions. Prahalad, bound by his word, gave his merits away. As soon as merit moved from Prahalad to Indra, Lakshmi also moved from Prahalad's side to Indra's side.

In the epic Ramayana, Ravana, king of the rakhasas, has physical power or strength. He has twenty arms and ten heads. With brute force, he overpowers his brother Kubera and drives him out of the golden island-city of Lanka and lays claim to kingdom and throne. With brute force, he abducts the wife of Ram, prince of Ayodhya. Thus Lakshmi comes to Ravana by force.

In the epic Mahabharata, Duryodhana, eldest of the Kauravas, is shrewd and guileful. He uses cunning to defeat his cousins, the five Pandavas, who are much stronger than him and who he feels are rivals to the throne of Hastinapur which he is convinced is his birthright. First, Duryodhana tries to get rid of the Pandavas by gifting them a palace of lac, which he sets afire while they are asleep. Unfortunately, this plan fails. Later he invites the Pandavas

Jain manuscript showing Lakshmi as Shri

to a gambling match and defeats them by getting his uncle, Shakuni, master of the dice, to play on his behalf. In exchange for their freedom, Pandavas have to forfeit rights over their land for thirteen years. Thus Lakshmi comes to the Kauravas by guile.

But Lakshmi acquired through strength or guile can never be retained. Someone who is stronger or more shrewd always comes along and claims our Lakshmi. Thus Ravana meets his match in Ram, the prince of Ayodhya, who defeats him in battle. And Duryodhana finds his match in Krishna, the wily charioteer, who helps the Pandavas outsmart the cunning Kauravas. Indra is never able to keep Lakshmi by his side for long, as there is always a stronger or smarter asura who comes along.

In the early part of the Vedas indicated by Brahmana texts, we find hymns and rituals about acquiring and celebrating wealth that take the form of cows, horses, grain, gold, children. Wealth is seen as ushering in happiness. In the latter part of the Vedas indicated by the Aranyaka and Upanishad texts, we find a great discomfort with wealth. Wealth is seen as something that also brings with it a great deal of unhappiness: the envy of neighbours, loss of friends, quarrels within family. This shift in thought between early and later Vedic periods on the nature of wealth is reflected in how Indra is positioned. Indra is the great warrior king of the Vedas, but in the Puranas, he is insecure and helpless, constantly seeking the help of Brahma, Vishnu and Shiva.

Giving up wealth simply because its arrival can cause unhappiness is not the answer. What is, then? This enquiry leads us to Vedanta, which explores the relationship between mind and

Stone sculpture of Jyestha, elder sister of Lakshmi

property. Vedanta means philosophy that was milked out of the Vedas. It was communicated to the common man through the stories of the Puranas.

In the Puranas, we learn of Lakshmi's elder sister, Jyestha, also known as Alakshmi, who always accompanies her. She is the goddess of strife. She is the reason why the prosperity of Lakshmi is never accompanied by peace. The only way to get peace into the household is to discover and invoke either Shiva or Vishnu. When Lakshmi accompanies Shiva or Vishnu, then Alakshmi does not accompany Lakshmi, and so wealth is not accompanied by quarrels.

Shiva is a hermit and does not care for wealth. But when he gets married to Parvati, she forces him to pay attention to the needs of his followers, the ganas, and his devotees, the bhaktas. She makes him aware that those around him are not tapasvins like him; they have desires and hungers that need satisfaction. They need food. Shiva satisfies the desires and hungers of his ganas and his bhaktas through his children, Kartikeya and Ganesha. While the mighty Kartikeya provides protection, Ganesha provides prosperity.

Ganesha's form evokes Lakshmi. His head is of a white elephant, like those that raise their trunks and spray water on Lakshmi. His corpulent form evokes Kubera, the god of treasures. He rides a rat, that enemy of farmers, and around his belly is a snake, symbol of regeneration, much desired by farmers. That natural enemies, the rat and snake, are both beside Ganesha reveals a desire to keep away the strife of the jungle and create a culture of peace. In imagery, Lakshmi is often shown beside Ganesha, even though traditionally Lakshmi and Ganesha belong to rival religious sects, the Vaishnavas and the Shaivas. Together, Lakshmi and Ganesha evoke affluence and abundance.

Poster art of Lakshmi with Ganesha

When Ravana drove Kubera out of Lanka, Kubera moved north and sought refuge in Mount Kailas, abode of Shiva. There he built the city of A-Lanka, the opposite of Lanka, which later came to be known as Alaka. It was even more prosperous than Lanka. But Kubera noticed that Shiva was not interested in his wealth. He did not understand how the ascetic Shiva could possibly satisfy the hunger of Ganesha, who clearly looked like one who enjoyed food. So Kubera invited Ganesha to his house to eat 'to his heart's content'. Ganesha accepted the invitation. But Kubera soon realised that Ganesha's appetite was huge: he could eat more than what Kubera could provide. Before long he had consumed all the food in Kubera's house. He even ate all the food that Kubera's wealth could buy. Reduced to poverty, Kubera begged Ganesha to stop, but Ganesha reminded Kubera of his promise to feed him to 'his heart's content'. Kubera realised he had made a huge mistake. Finally, Ganesha said, 'Now you understand why I stay with Shiva and not you. You seek to satisfy my hunger, but Shiva helps me outgrow my hunger. The more food you serve, the more my hunger is fuelled; thus my hunger remains insatiable. The only solution then is to outgrow hunger, for which I need Shiva.'

This story reveals a philosophy very different from the one found in the early Vedas. The point of life is not to satisfy hunger, the point of life is to outgrow hunger. Animals do not eat more than what they need, but humans have an eternal craving for more and more wealth. This craving is insatiable. So rather than trying to satisfy it with food, it is more important to destroy the hunger itself. This does not mean rejecting Lakshmi; it means putting Lakshmi in perspective.

There is a vast difference between real hunger and invented

Poster art of Lakshmi with Kubera and Nidhi

hunger. Human imagination blurs the line between need and want. That is why the arrival of Lakshmi is always associated with Alakshmi, goddess of quarrels. If we are able to outgrow our own hunger, without denying her value to the world, then we are able to share Lakshmi with others. When we share, there are fewer quarrels: Lakshmi comes without Alakshmi. To be able to share Lakshmi, we need to discover Shiva and Shakti.

Indra is so focused on Lakshmi, or rather Sachi, his wife, that he is indifferent to Alakshmi. He takes no steps to protect himself from the envy and rage of those around him. Naturally, fortune and happiness are short-lived. Eventually, inevitably, while he is busy with his wine and women and other excesses, his enemies lay siege to Swarga and declare war.

One day, Lakshmi leaves Swarga in a huff when Indra insults her: in a drunken state, he throws a garland of lotus flowers gifted to him to the ground, allowing it to be trampled by elephants. This disrespect shown to wealth and affluence is something Lakshmi does not like, so she dissolves herself in the ocean of milk.

With the disappearance of Lakshmi, the world becomes gloomy, and Indra's paradise loses its affluence. The wish-fulfilling cow stops giving milk, the wish-fulfilling tree stops bearing fruit, the wish-fulfilling gem loses its shine, and the wish-fulfilling pot becomes empty. The only way to get Lakshmi back to Swarga is by churning her out from the ocean of milk. So Indra goes to his father Brahma for help, and Brahma directs him to Vishnu.

Vishnu advises that Indra first make friends with the asuras, as a counter-force is required to churn the ocean. He then forms the

Mysore painting of the churning of the ocean of milk

churning tool by using Meru, the king of mountains, as a spindle, and Vasuki, the king of serpents, as a rope. Akupara, the king of turtles, a form of Vishnu himself, keeps this aloft. The churning begins with the devas holding the tail-end of Vasuki and the asuras holding the neck-end. When the devas pull, the asuras let go. When the asuras pull, the devas let go.

The churning goes on for eons. And finally from the waters arises Lakshmi, along with all the treasures of paradise. Along with her come Kalpataru, Kamadhenu, Chintamani and Akshaya-patra, symbols of wealth. Also with her are the elephant Airavata and the flying horse Ucchaishrava, both white as milk, symbols of royal power. Also with her is Rambha, the most beautiful damsel, who is well-versed in all forms of pleasure, and Soma, the moon-god, the most handsome and romantic of men.

Lakshmi also brings with her a pot of amrita, the nectar of immortality. This is sought by everyone, but Vishnu tricks the asuras and ensures only the devas get to drink the amrita. The devas, rendered immortal, then rise to their heaven with Lakshmi and everything that brings prosperity, power and pleasure.

But there is one change. Lakshmi herself chooses to go to Vishnu. She is drawn to him. This is significant: it establishes Vishnu as superior to Indra. Indra may have defeated the asuras, but it is Vishnu who enabled the victory. And even though Vishnu enabled the victory, he does not claim the much sought-after amrita.

They may seem similar, but there is a vast difference between Indra and Vishnu. This difference is not about form, but thought. Indra's name alludes to 'indriyas', or sense organs. Indra symbolises the mind that enjoys pleasure, hoards wealth, and feels constantly threatened by others. He only wants to satisfy his needs

Poster art showing Lakshmi choosing Vishnu as her groom

and wants. By contrast, Vishnu is concerned about the needs and wants of others.

Like Shiva, Vishnu wants to outgrow the world; but his method is different. While Shiva withdraws from society to outgrow his hunger, Vishnu engages with society to outgrow his hunger. He strives hard to help humans discover their dharma.

Dharma means potential. Every creature has to do what they are supposed to do, what they are capable of. It is the dharma of fire to burn, of water to flow, of trees to grow and bear fruit, of animals to run towards food and mates and away from predators. But what is human potential? Is it to create/hoard/distribute wealth to satisfy one's own hunger like Indra, or is it to outgrow hunger like Shiva? Humans are not clear about what path to take. That is why we need Vishnu.

Vishnu balances the shortcomings of Brahma's sons such as Indra with the possibility offered by Shiva. He knows that humans have the capacity to satisfy their own hunger as well as the hunger of others. They also have the capacity to outgrow — and enable others to outgrow — their own hunger. He works towards enabling people to become aware of this capacity, help themselves by helping others. And he does this in the most counter-intuitive of ways.

Superficially, it seems as though Vishnu favours devas over asuras. But a closer observation reveals it is not as simple as it looks. He is granting devas immortality. Why then is Indra still craving for Lakshmi? Should he not be happy as he no longer has to fear death and hence has no real need for Lakshmi? Should he not be content? But he is not: the hunger for Lakshmi continues.

And ironically, Lakshmi, grabbed from the asuras, rejects the

Stone image of Lakshmi-Varaha from Mammalapuram, Tamil Nadu

devas, and follows Vishnu. Vishnu has that which no one else has.

Yes, Vishnu is stronger than anyone else. When Hiranayaksha drags the earth under the sea, Vishnu descends into the waters as a boar, gores him to death with his mighty tusks, places the earth-goddess on his snout and brings her back to the surface.

Yes, Vishnu can outsmart the over-smart. When Hiranya-kashipu secures a boon that makes it impossible for him to be killed during the day or night, inside a dwelling or outside, on the ground or in the air, by a weapon or a tool, by a human or an animal, Vishnu takes the form of a monster (neither lion nor human), and kills him at twilight (neither day nor night), on the threshold (neither inside nor outside), on his lap (neither on the ground nor in the air), using his claws (neither a weapon nor a tool).

But like Shiva, Vishnu knows that food does not satisfy hunger. It only amplifies hunger. One can never satiate human needs and wants. He demonstrates this in the story of Vaman. When Bali tries to solve the world's problems through charity, Vishnu takes the form of a dwarf, asks for three paces of land, and on obtaining it, transforms into a giant who, with two paces, covers the whole world, and with the third step pushes Bali under the ground. Vishnu demonstrates that the world is infinite and human resources are finite. We cannot solve human problems with things. We need to pay attention to thoughts. Only when humans expand their mind can they recognise their own fears and empathise with the fears of those around them. To do so is human dharma.

This focus on thoughts rather than things is what makes Vishnu attractive to Lakshmi. She sits next to him when he is Varaha, admiring the thought behind his strength. She sits next to him when

Poster art of Lakshmi-Narasimha

he is Narasimha, admiring the thought behind his cleverness. She sits next to him when he is Hayagriva, the horse-headed one, who explains the secret of the scriptures to the sages. And this secret has nothing to do with matter, it has to do with the human mind. While Western philosophy focuses only on science and society, Indian philosophy puts greater emphasis on psychology. In the human mind is the seed of all human problems and all human solutions.

Lakshmi has two forms: Bhu-devi and Sri-devi. Bhu-devi is the earth-goddess and embodies tangible wealth like food. Sri-devi is associated with intangible wealth or glamour. One can say Bhu-devi is natural wealth and Sri-devi is cultural wealth. In south Indian temples these two forms of Lakshmi are seen beside images of Vishnu.

In the Puranas, Bhu-devi is often visualised as a cow. The story goes that a king called Vena plundered the earth so much that the rishis had to intervene and kill this greedy king. They churned his corpse and from the purified remains created a new king, Prithu. Prithu was a form of Vishnu. He discovered that the earth had run away in the form of a cow, so he pursued her with his bow and arrow, threatening to strike her if she did not stop and allow his subjects to milk her. 'If you kill me, the world will cease to exist,' she cried. 'But if you cannot be milked, the world cannot survive,' argued Prithu. So finally, assured that he would protect her and not let anyone plunder her, Bhu-devi let herself be milked by all living creatures under the watchful eye of Prithu.

As Prithu, Vishnu declared that the kings of the earth would

Miniature painting of Prithu chasing the earth-cow

be guardians of Bhu-devi, and that he himself would descend on earth if she was troubled. He becomes the Go-pala, or caretaker of the earth-cow Go-mata.

In the *Bhagavata Purana,* Bhu-devi comes weeping to Vishnu and complains about the weight of greedy kings that she has to bear and begs him to relieve her burden. And so Vishnu descends as Parashuram, Ram and Krishna to kill all the greedy kings of the world. Thus the avatars of Vishnu are meant to secure Lakshmi. She is under Vishnu's protection.

In the stories of his mortal avatars – Parashuram, Ram and Krishna – Vishnu never claims ownership of Lakshmi, even in situations when he is 'entitled' to her.

Parashuram fights brutally to reclaim his mother-cow from the clutches of Kartaviryarjuna, who tries to claim her forcibly. He even enforces his mother's fidelity by beheading her on his father's orders when she has adulterous thoughts. Both actions are done out of obedience for the father, and not for his own benefit.

In the next avatar, the 'rule' of obedience to the father is questioned as it creates crisis in culture, depriving the kingdom of a good king. As Ram, Vishnu is tranquil when his father asks him to give up claims over Ayodhya. He is equally tranquil when the kingdom is returned to him and he is crowned its king. Ram's relationship with Sita reveals the complexity of God's relationship with Goddess in a world that speaks of 'duties' and 'rights'. Ram dutifully accepts Sita as his wife when her father offers him her hand in marriage; he allows her to follow him to the forest during his exile, even though he would be more than happy if she stayed back in the palace; he rescues her from Ravana's captivity but does not reclaim her, letting her choose him over freedom; and when his

Modern painting of Lakshmi-Hayagriva

subjects gossip about her fidelity, he abandons her in the forest. At one level, Ram's treatment of Sita is disturbing, as he seems almost indifferent to her needs. At another level, he claims no 'rights' over her. And when it comes to 'duties', he chooses his duty as king over duty as husband, unquestioningly following the royal codes of conduct. This demands great sacrifice. When asked to remarry, however, he chooses to stay single, rejecting his 'right to remarry' and his 'duty as king', thereby expressing his affection for the Goddess and his understanding of her: culture needs her, but she does not need culture.

In Krishna's story, the Goddess takes many forms. She is Radha to Krishna before his marriage; she loves him even though she belongs to another, thus defying all cultural norms. She is Rukmini who defies her father and elopes with him to Dwarka. She is Satyabhama who obeys her father and marries him, but constantly reminds him that it is her wealth, not his intelligence alone, that makes him an influential member of the Yadava clan. Krishna treats both the poor Rukmini and the rich Satyabhama with affection, for he is worldly-wise and values both: the love of Rukmini and the wealth of Satyabhama. When Krishna meets Sudama, he wishes to offer all his wealth to his poor friend, but Satyabhama stops him from excessive generosity, reminding him that there are many others in need of charity. Finally, the Goddess takes the form of Draupadi, who is helpless and abused despite having five husbands to protect her. Her husbands, the Pandavas, are described as Indras reborn. She needs Vishnu to help her and he does so as Krishna even though he is not obliged to do so by any social law or custom. He does so out of love.

Unlike Indra, who only sees Lakshmi as pleasure, Vishnu sees

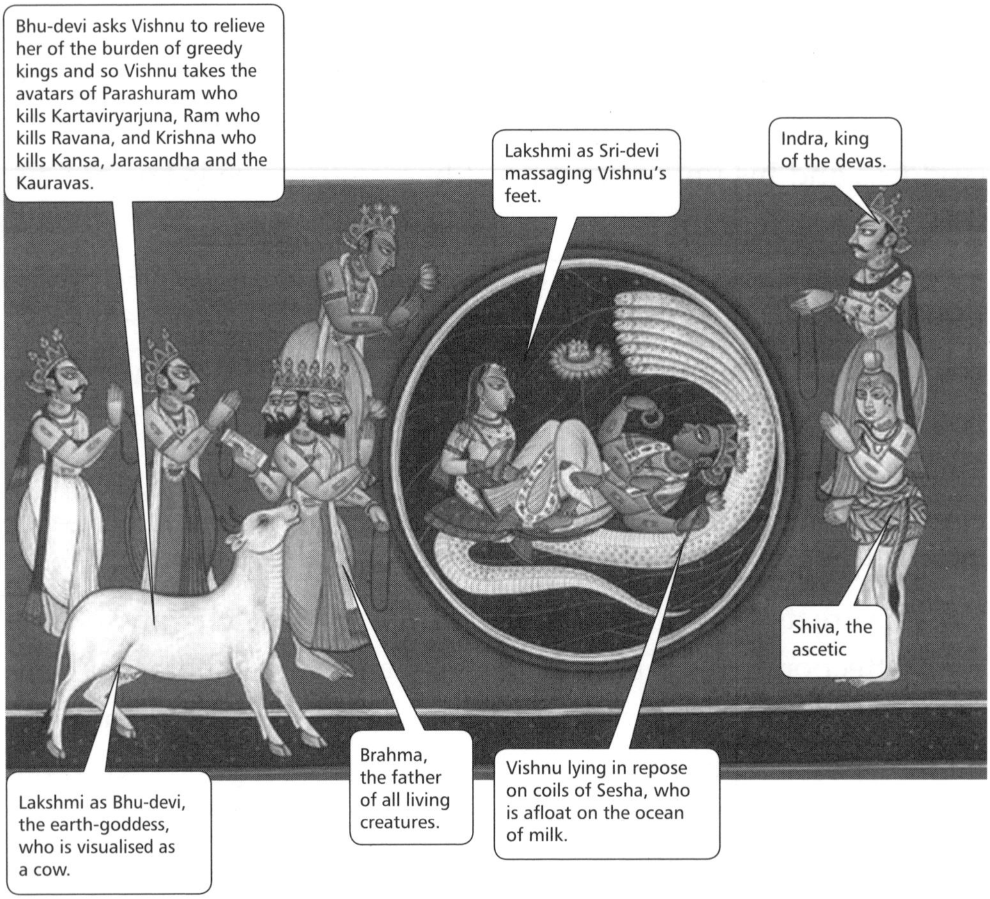

Miniature painting of earth-cow approaching Vishnu for help

Lakshmi as his responsibility. Vishnu seeks to create an ecosystem where Lakshmi is not held captive; instead she is distributed and celebrated by all.

The story goes that humans are in debt because they milk the earth. This debt gets repaid in blood when Parashuram kills Kartaviryarjuna, Ram kills Ravana, and Krishna kills Kansa, Jarasandha and oversees the destruction of the Kauravas. Kali spreads her tongue to quench her thirst resulting from excessive milking of her resources by humanity.

As Hinduism made its journey from Vedic ritualism to Puranic devotion, it became increasingly monastic. This meant that the yogi, one who does not care for wealth, was given more respect in society than a bhogi, one who enjoys wealth. In such a society, Lakshmi was seen as the source of all problems. Rather than taking responsibility for their own inadequacies, human society blamed Lakshmi for the conflicts of society.

This tension between the yogi and the bhogi is a constant theme in the Puranas. The yogi Shiva is turned into the bhogi Shankara when he marries Parvati. The bhogi Indra learns from the yogi Vishnu how to transform rana-bhoomi or battleground into ranga-bhoomi or playground. Similar tensions can be seen in temple lore, where the language is regional, and the themes more practical.

The following is an Odiya story which is part of the temple lore of Puri Jagannath temple where Krishna Jagannath is worshipped along with his brother Balabhadra and his sister Subhadra.

One day, Balabhadra sees Lakshmi entering the house of a sweeper woman. He declares that she has been contaminated and

Lakshmi as she is worshipped in Puri, Odisha

orders his younger brother not to let her into the house. Krishna obeys and shuts the door of the temple. In the days that follow, to the great alarm of the divine siblings, no food is offered to them. On enquiry, they discover there is no food being cooked in the kitchen as all vegetables and fruits and cereals and pulses and spices have disappeared from the pantry and the market. There is not even a drop of water to drink. The siblings trace this catastrophe to their rejection of Lakshmi. Eventually Krishna apologises to his wife and begs her to return to the temple.

In this story, Krishna's ascetic brother, the yogi Balabhadra, learns that notions of contamination and pollution make no sense to the goddess of wealth. These are artificial cultural norms created by humans to satisfy their craving for hierarchy. Food will satisfy without discrimination the hunger of all, be it a sweeper, a king or a god. In other words, food is satya, truth independent of human opinion. Notions of contamination, which is the hallmark of the caste system, is mithya, dependent on human opinion. When we discover that Lakshmi does not discriminate between saint and thief, that all hierarchies are manmade creations, then Lakshmi becomes a tool for liberation.

The following is a Telugu tale from one of the richest temples of India, the temple of Tirupati Balaji that enshrines Vishnu on earth.

The sage Bhrigu, a yogi, decided to pay a visit to Brahma, Shiva and Vishnu. He found Brahma too busy conducting a yagna with Saraswati to pay him attention, so he cursed Brahma that he would not be worshipped at all. He found Shiva too busy being intimate with Shakti to pay him attention. This time, his anger was a little less, and so he said Shiva would be worshipped, but not as he looks — only as an abstract symbol, the linga. He then moved

Images of Vishnu as bhogi

to the ocean of milk, to Vaikuntha, convinced that Vishnu would surely pay him attention. But there he found Vishnu sleeping, his feet being massaged by Lakshmi. Furious that he mattered to none in the trinity, Bhrigu kicked Vishnu on his chest, where is located Srivatsa, the symbol of Lakshmi. Vishnu did not get upset; he understood Bhrigu's frustration and apologised to the sage, and checked if Bhrigu had hurt his foot while kicking his chest. Watching Vishnu touch his feet, Bhrigu was happy. Then realisation dawned as to how foolish he was being: though he claimed to be a yogi, his attention-seeking behaviour revealed he was actually a bhogi.

Lakshmi did not appreciate Vishnu's servility, whatever his reason. She was furious that Vishnu did not punish the sage for insulting the Srivatsa. She walked out of Vaikuntha in a huff and went down to earth. Vishnu followed her, desperate to bring her back, for Vaikuntha cannot remain Vaikuntha without Lakshmi. He decided to stay on earth until Lakshmi agreed to return. But he found no house; devotees would give him shelter until someone richer or more powerful came along. Finally, he saw the seven hills that reminded him of the seven hoods of his serpent Sesha on whose coils he reclined on the ocean of milk. This was Tirumala, the sacred hill. Homesick, he wished to settle here, but for that he had to marry the local princess Padmavati, born of a lotus flower. Her father, the local king, demanded a huge bridal price. Without Lakshmi by his side, Vishnu was the impoverished Daridra-Narayana, and so he had no choice but to take a huge loan from Kubera. This narrative demonstrates the value of wealth in society; even Vishnu needs wealth to get himself a wife and home on earth. One who rejects Lakshmi cannot expect to have a home or a spouse.

Popular images of the rage and reconciliation of Lakshmi

News of Vishnu's marriage to Padmavati upset Lakshmi who came to the wedding and demanded her place in Vishnu's chest. So Vishnu expanded his chest to accommodate his two wives. He placed the celestial Lakshmi (Sri-devi) on the left side of his chest, near his heart, and the terrestrial Padmavati (Bhu-devi) on the right.

This Vishnu at Tirumala is trapped and needs the help of his devotees to repay his debt, so that he can return to Vaikuntha. He is called Venkat, he who can destroy (kata) bondage (vem), for in exchange of the wealth received, he grants his devotees the wisdom of yoga that explains the relationship one should have with wealth in order to be truly happy. This is further demonstrated in the ritual of giving wealth to transform Daridra-Narayana (the poor Vishnu) into Lakshmi-Narayana (the rich Vishnu): when Lakshmi is used to enable others to repay their debts, Vaikuntha is established and Lakshmi becomes a tool for liberation.

6. Saraswati's Secret

Imagination can expand or contract the mind

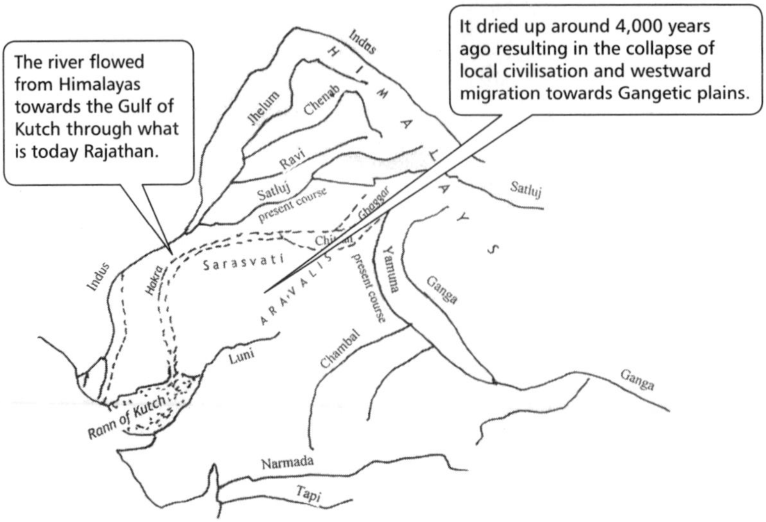

The now-dry river Saraswati referred to in the *Rig Veda*

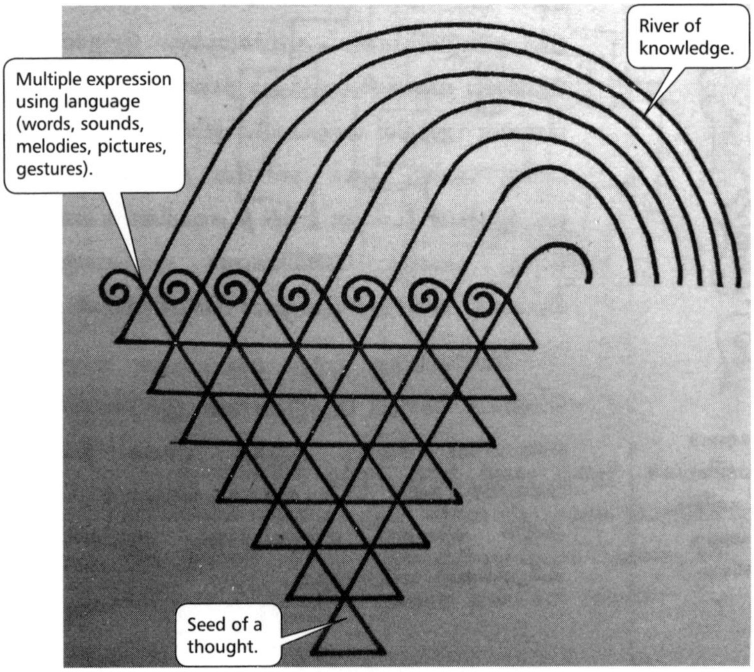

Symbol of Saraswati used in schools

Experts on the Vedas often say how the Saraswati has dried up. No one is sure what this means exactly. Does this refer to a river that flowed four thousand years ago in Punjab, Sindh and Rajasthan, on whose banks many of the hymns of the *Rig Veda* came to be composed? Or does it refer to the metaphorical river of language and imagination that is used more to control the world, rather than break free from fear? No one is sure. Different scholars approach Vedic verses differently, either literally or symbolically.

In the Puranas, Saraswati is a well-defined goddess. Her stories are rare, though always related to language. The devas, for example, invoke her just when the demon Kumbhakarna is about to ask Brahma for a boon and request her to twist the rakshasa's tongue so that instead of Indra-asan (seat of Indra), he asks for Nidra-asan (sleep).

In these Puranas, Saraswati is identified as the first creation of Brahma, even the first woman created by Brahma. Brahma gets infatuated with her. Such 'incestuous' affection is frowned upon and Rudra-Shiva, who embodies renunciation, either beheads Brahma or simply pins him to the sky to stop him from pursuing her. Like Vedic hymns, this Puranic story can be seen literally or symbolically. Symbolically, it refers to the tension between a creator claiming ownership over his creation and the renouncer destroying this relationship and advocating detachment. The daughter is sometimes called Shatarupa, she of many forms. When Brahma steps back and observes his creation, not with the desire to control it but from the desire to understand it, he realises it reflects his own mind. His creation is a mirror that reflects his

Poster art showing Brahma and Saraswati

own personality. Shatarupa then becomes his teacher Saraswati, she who flows in the mind.

Some sociologists are of the opinion that the absence of Brahma temples in later Hinduism was a symbolic rejection of the old Vedic way that was highly materialistic. The rise of Vishnu and Shiva temples marks a shift in thought in Hinduism. In the Puranas, Saraswati who shuns the vile Brahma becomes consort of Vishnu according to Vaishnavas, the companion of Ganesha according to Shaivas and the daughter of Shakti according to Shaktas. In the new form of Hinduism, where answers were sought in temples, beyond materialism, but always through materialism, the all-male triad of Brahma, Vishnu and Shiva was replaced by the triad of Devi, Vishnu and Shiva.

While Shiva is commonly paired with Shakti who is Durga/Kali/Gauri, and Vishnu is paired with Lakshmi, it is not clear who Saraswati should be paired with. To maintain symmetry between the male triad (Shiva, Vishnu, Brahma) and the female triad (Durga, Lakshmi, Saraswati), it is common to link Brahma with Saraswati. The explanation given for this is that the creator needs knowledge, the sustainer needs wealth and the destroyer needs power. This is a more convenient explanation than an accurate one, for everyone knows that all three resources are needed for all three jobs. To assume that you can create with knowledge alone, without wealth and power, or you can sustain only with wealth, without knowledge or power, is fantastic to say the least.

In medieval times, it was common to show Lakshmi and Saraswati as the two consorts of Vishnu, and Shakti as his sister.

Folk Bengal art showing Saraswati with Kartikeya

Pahari miniature painting showing Ganesha with Saraswati

The rival sect of Shiva-worshippers also appropriated Lakshmi and Saraswati by placing them on either side of Ganesha, Shiva's more worldly son. As Ganesha's consorts, they are more popularly known as Riddhi (goddess of material treasures) and Siddhi (goddess of mental powers). In Bengal, Lakshmi is associated with the food-loving Ganesha, who is associated with learned Brahmins; and Saraswati with the art-loving Kartikeya, associated with affluent landowners or zamindars.

Despite being linked to Brahma, Vishnu, Ganesha and Kartikeya, images of Saraswati with a male consort are rare. She is shown as aloof and distant, always alone, content in her own company, an indicator of true wisdom. Unlike other goddesses who turn 'hot' and fiery and dangerous when kept away from matrimony and maternity, Saraswati remains calm and composed despite her isolation. A cynic may equate Saraswati's white sari not with asceticism but with widowhood, revealing the loneliness of women especially, but also men, who are extremely intelligent or intellectual or smart.

Saraswati, like Lakshmi, is essentially an independent goddess. Her origins can be traced to the four thousand-year-old *Rig Samhita*. There she shares her name with the river Saraswati and her qualities with Vak, goddess of speech, language and meaning. She is sometimes also linked to Gayatri, the goddess of Vedic hymns and melodies.

The Vedas paid great attention to language. Language was at one time called 'brahman', which etymologically means that which expands (brah, in Sanskrit) the mind (manas). Later, the word

Poster of Sharada, patron goddess of Shankar-acharya

brahman came to mean divinity. Language is the one thing that distinguishes humans from other animals. Animals communicate with each other but they are just signals; human language is more complex, allowing people to explore and express abstract concepts, intangible ideas, such as 'past', 'present', 'beyond', 'love' and 'friendship'.

Language can be expressed using gestures (mudras), using speech (vak) and of course, script. The vowels or matras were associated with goddesses, the Matrikas. And early Indian scripts, Brahmi and Sharada, were both personified as women and goddesses. Brahmi was the daughter of the Jain Tirthankara Rishabha, to whom he bequeathed the first script. Sharada became another form of Saraswati and Vak, who was especially worshipped by Adi Shankara, the great 8th century Vedanta scholar, who probably read works of earlier philosophers in the Sharada script.

Language emerges from imagination and it also expands imagination. Imagination is one thing that animals do not have, at least not on the scale of humans. Imagination is fluid (saras), and can either be contained as a lake (sarovar) or made to flow like a river (sarita). From saras, comes Saraswati.

Imagination allows humans to travel through space without moving and through time in a single moment. Imagination allows humans to conjure up worlds that do not exist. Humans communicate these thoughts through language. Saraswati is the goddess of fluid thoughts and words, an exclusively human goddess, who grants humanity to humans. Perhaps that is why Hindus paint their forehead with sacred marks, for the head contains the brain, the home of Saraswati. A dot, or the bindu, in

Varied attributes of Saraswati

the centre of the forehead is an indicator of human potential, our ability to make sense of the world, and solve any of its problems.

Because Saraswati enables us to understand and appreciate nature, she eventually became the goddess of arts, associated with literature and music, and holds in her hands a book and a lute (vina, in Sanskrit). She is even called Veda-mata, the mother of the Vedas. She is also the mother of svaras (musical notes) and ragas (melodies).

In imagery, Saraswati is often associated with a goose (hamsa) because legend has it that a goose can separate milk from a mixture of milk and water. In other words, it can separate truth (milk) from falsehood (water), making it the symbol of analysis. Saraswati is also associated with the heron, which is the symbol of concentration. And in modern calendar art, with a peacock which does not spread its feathers in her presence as it knows that humility is the true measure of wisdom.

She is associated with white and transparent things to indicate her purity. She is associated with white champa flowers and the white autumn moon and white transparent crystal beads.

She is often invoked during Vasant, or springtime, because the season of spring inspires poets to compose songs. In this month, she is dressed in bright yellow clothes, the colour of mustard flowers.

Many scholars trace the modern Saraswati to Tara, a Buddhist goddess who had a major role to play in the transformation of Buddhism. Buddha was initially uncomfortable with the female

Tibetan painting of the Buddhist Tara

form and women in general. Women were seen as daughters of Mara, the demon of desire. Gradually Buddha softened, especially after he saw the sorrow of his step-mother when his father died, and so he allowed women to be part of the monastic order. Still women played a secondary role. With the rise of the Mahayana, the later school of Buddhism, the idea of a feminine force that empathises with humanity and is less intellectual in its approach emerged. This was Tara. Like Parvati, Tara is known for her ability to turn the indifferent monk into an engaged saviour. Like Lakshmi, Tara holds a lotus in her hand. But she is, like Saraswati, renowned as the embodiment of pragnya, or wisdom.

Saraswati was closely associated with dancers, musicians and courtesans as she was seen as the mother of the arts and theatre. Through songs and plays and literature, she could evoke a variety of aesthetic experiences (rasa) in the audience that could grant both entertainment and enlightenment at the same time. This is one reason why, in Bengal, she was associated with Kartikeya, who was visualised as an affluent rasik, a connoisseur of the arts who frequented the houses of talented singers and dancers.

But as monastic orders rose in India, knowledge was divided into pure knowledge that grants spiritual bliss (yoga), and impure knowledge that arouses the senses and generates wealth (bhoga). The former was associated with priests, philosophers, ascetics and devotional poet-saints, while the latter was associated with entertainers, dancers, singers, musicians and performers. The former came to be more associated with Saraswati, and the latter more with Vidya-Lakshmi, vocational and transactional knowledge. This is one reason why 'commercial' artists have historically been frowned upon. Art for them is about making

Odisha patta painting showing Maha-vidya Baglamukhi

money and not about expanding the mind.

This disdain for the commercial artist is the reason why the 'nat' (entertainer) or the 'ganika' (courtesan) was always looked upon with suspicion. This suspicion combined with the puritanical nature of the Victorian era lead to the banning of devadasi practices and of classification of the caste of entertainers as 'criminal tribes' in British India.

In Vaishnava literature, Lakshmi became bhoga-patni, who entraps with pleasure, and Saraswati became moksha-patni, who liberates with wisdom. Stories emerged in Bhagavat parampara of how Krishna has to balance the demands of his rich wife, Satyabhama, and his gentle, wise wife, Rukmini. For the audience, the rich Satyabhama who dominates and shows off her wealth is Lakshmi, while the poor Rukmini who has nothing except devotion and wisdom is Saraswati.

One belief related to Saraswati that is common in almost every Hindu household is this: she never stays in the same house as Lakshmi, as they quarrel all the time.

The difference between the two goddesses is stark. Lakshmi is dressed as a bride, in red, embellished with ornaments; Saraswati is dressed as a widow, in white, with no regard for ornamentation even though artists deck her with crystal beads and white flowers. Lakshmi is attractive while Saraswati is aloof. Lakshmi comes and goes on a whim, but can be held in place using force and cunning. Saraswati comes only with great effort, but once she comes she does not leave.

In one folk tale, tired of the quarrels between his two wives,

Pala sculpture from Bengal showing Vishnu with Lakshmi and Saraswati

Vishnu separates them by placing Saraswati on his tongue and Lakshmi in his heart (or some say, his feet). Thus he gets the best of both — the invisible Saraswati and the visible Lakshmi.

The quarrel revolves around this one single idea: what matters more in worldly life, wealth or knowledge. This quarrel can be traced to the conflict between three major Vedic communities: the brahmins who were keepers and transmitters of Vedic knowledge, the kshatriyas who were warriors and so held bows and rode chariots, and the vaniks or vaishyas who were traders and so had access to wealth. In other words this conflict was not just about Saraswati of the brahmins and Lakshmi of the vaishyas but also Durga of the kshatriyas. It asks a deeper, philosophical question: what really matters in society — knowledge, wealth or power.

At the root of this conflict is the human desire to dominate. Why do humans seek to dominate? Animals dominate so as to get more access to food and mates. They cannot help themselves; it is in-built as part of nature's survival strategy. Humans however have the choice whether to dominate or not. And this choice comes from imagination, from Saraswati.

With imagination, humans come up with ideas and inventions that enable them to create surplus food. So there is really no need for a pecking order — there is enough for everyone to go around. And yet humans want to dominate. This comes from a deeper anxiety, a unique human anxiety — the quest for identity. Who am I? This quest also comes from Saraswati.

Animals have no doubt about where they are in nature's food chain and pecking order. But the imagination of humans creates doubts. Every human being can imagine themselves in a particular way. But those around may not imagine them in the same way. This

Poster of Gayatri, a personified Vedic hymn

creates conflict. We seek to impose and assert our imagining of ourselves on others. We want others to see us as we see ourselves.

In early societies, strength and cunning was used to dominate. But later, with surplus wealth, the idea of property emerged. He who had more property could dominate even the strong and the smart. Property could be inherited, and so one did not really need strength, skill or even cunning to acquire it. Social laws and concepts of ethics and morality ensured no one could usurp someone else's property. This secured the wealth of the wealthy. So, naturally, those who inherited wealth did not care much for knowledge. They did not even care for strength, skill or social status. With wealth everything could be bought – even people who were strong, skilled, talented and beautiful.

One group of people suffered greatly because of the rise in the importance of property. They were the keepers of Vedic lore. Vedic hymns had to be transmitted orally; they could not be written down as scripts could not adequately capture the intonations of Vedic mantras. This meant the entire day was spent chanting hymns using various techniques known as pada-patha. The focus remained so much on chanting that even understanding the hymns was ignored. Such a community dedicated to securing Vedic lore had no time to generate wealth for themselves. Wealth came only in the form of gifts and donations. Thus the idea emerged that where there is Lakshmi, there is no Saraswati, and where there is Saraswati, there is no Lakshmi.

Over time, Vedic priests created vocations for themselves, became astrologers, grammarians, temple priests, scribes and bureaucrats to generate Lakshmi for their households, but the relationship with wealth remained a tricky one. It was seen as

Mysore painting of Saraswati, the goddess of the arts

corrupting and distracting. Strangely, no one noticed that even knowledge could be corrupting and distracting. Because those who were too busy memorising and transmitting the Vedic hymns and rituals remained clueless about their meaning or significance.

Vedic knowledge is all about expanding the mind, outgrowing fear, in the quest for self-realisation. As long as the mind is contracted, there is fear, and hence the desire to dominate. While the kshastriyas dominated society using power (Durga), and the vaishyas dominated society using their wealth (Lakshmi), the brahmins dominated society by claiming to be 'purer' than others as they were keepers of esoteric knowledge (Saraswati). This hierarchy of purity is unique to Indian society and it wreaked havoc in Indian society.

Everything that the brahmin could not partake of as the keeper of Vedic lore became a source of impurity: meat, alcohol, sexual pleasure, wealth, property, trade, even vocations that involved physical labour and contact with nature. So the purest man was one who shunned all things worldly and material. Impurity became contagious and so to establish purity, the brahmin avoided contact with all things 'impure'. He isolated himself from other communities and even from his own wife when she was menstruating with a feeling of superiority. This idea caught on and spread across all communities.

Everyone who wanted to climb up the social ladder realised it was possible to do so even without wealth and power or even knowledge, by simply embracing the concept of 'purity'. The pure could look down upon the impure. Eventually, communities or jatis started locating themselves on the purity hierarchy. On top were the brahmins. At the bottom were a whole bunch of professions

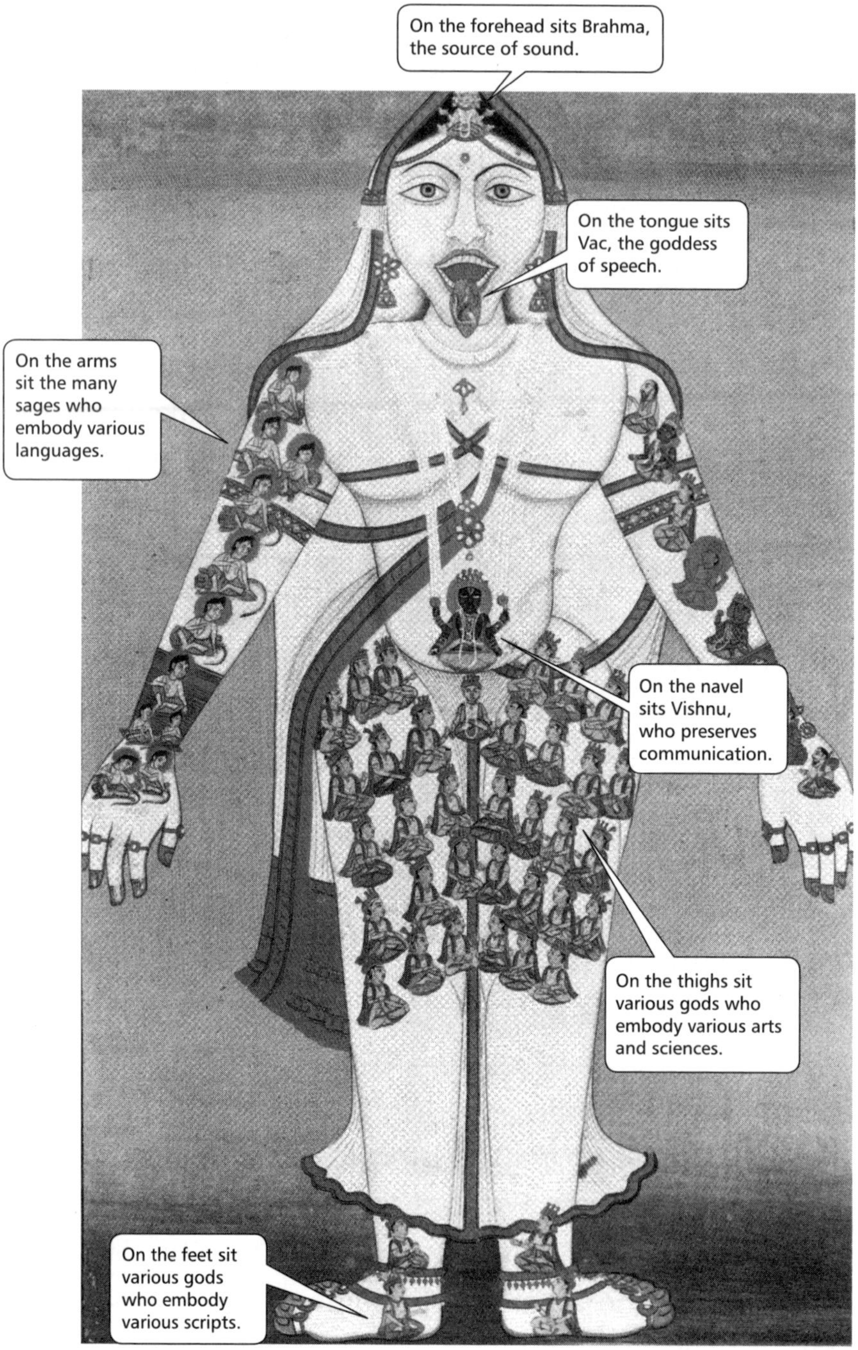

Cosmic form of Saraswati

such as tanners, cobblers, sweepers, toilet-cleaners, butchers, who were considered so impure that they were even denied access to the village well.

Thus, Saraswati who was supposed to expand the human mind and help humans discover atma, ended up becoming the cause of contracting the human mind and amplifying aham. Self-awareness was overshadowed with self-delusion. The draconian caste system became the hallmark of Hinduism. It continues to haunt Hinduism today as people continue to strive to be 'purer'.

To be pure is to assume there is dirt in the world. Dirt is a cultural concept, not a natural one. In Tantra, where Devi worship takes centre-stage, great value is therefore given to what is shunned by purity-conscious mainstream society. Thus, the Goddess is offered meat and alcohol and blood. Even menstrual blood, seen as dirty and polluting by most communities, is seen as sacred and auspicious. It is described, as everything else in nature, as valid (satyam), energising (shivam) and beautiful (sundaram).

To outgrow the human need to dominate using wealth, status, knowledge, beauty, success and notions of purity, is to truly let Saraswati flow in our minds.

7. Vitthai's Secret

Affection dissolves boundaries

Photograph of a statue of Vitthal, a form of Krishna worshipped in Maharashtra

In the 13th century, a young sage from Maharashtra called Dyaneshwar did something revolutionary for the times: he translated the Sanskrit *Bhagavad Gita* into the local tongue of Maharashtri Prakrit (old Marathi). But with one difference: while in the Sanskrit *Bhagavad Gita,* Krishna is the valorous masculine warrior-charioteer, in Dyaneshwar's *Dyaneshwari,* Krishna is Vitth-ai, or 'mother Vitthal'.

Vitthal, who is enshrined in Pandharpur, is the popular name of Krishna in Maharashtra. Dyaneshwar saw him in feminine terms. For him, Krishna was the affectionate cow who comforts the lost and frightened calf, Arjuna, with his milk of wisdom. He used other metaphors for Krishna, all feminine, like the mother turtle who watches over her baby turtles with loving sidelong glances. This idea of 'mother Krishna' was carried forward by other poet-saints of Maharashtra, like Janabai and Tukaram. For these poets, gender was but a tool to communicate a very particular emotion. Love and wisdom mattered more than Krishna's gender. And no one took offence.

This feminisation of the masculine is fairly common in Hindu mythology. Hypermasculine characteristics of a village god, like a moustache, diminish with the rise in his status. Features become gentle and soft. Muscles disappear.

This contrasts with the trend to masculinise the feminine in modern society. While feminism, in principle, has been about reclaiming humanity by restoring the balance of power between men and women, in popular culture, a feminist is often projected as one who does everything that a man can. Thus, for society to

Popular representation of the sun-god Surya and his wife Saranya

17th century image from Nepal, of Surya with his wives and charioteer

progress, women have to compete with men. It is a race where she, not he, has to catch up.

This anxiety can be traced to monotheistic religions such as Islam and Christianity, where God is avowedly masculine with no room for the feminine. The relationship between God and Goddess in the stories and rituals of Hindu mythology has always been tumultuous. But there was never a time when the Goddess was dismissed.

In the Vedas, the gods have gender and there is a clear preference for the male. There are many more hymns dedicated to male devatas such as Surya (sun), Indra (sky), Agni (fire), Marutta (storm), Soma (herb/moon), Varuna (order) and Mitra (pact) than female devatas such as Prithvi (earth), Saraswati (river), Ushas (dawn), Nritti (death), and Aranyani (forest). The male deities reside above the earth, in the sky, and are associated with cultural order, while the female deities are associated with the earth and natural order. There are invocations to male ancestors (pitrs) and prayers for male offspring (putra). The gender divide is clear.

In the Upanishads, however, the idea of a cosmic consciousness or brahman starts to become more important than gods and goddesses. Cosmic consciousness is identified with atma, consciousness of the individual. Both the cosmic brahman and individual atma are described as nirguna, without form, unfettered by the body, hence genderless. The Upanishads are also called Vedanta, the philosophy milked out of the Vedas.

But all talk of consciousness remained with the elite. The ordinary village folk preferred their grama-devas who satisfied their basic

Stone sculpture of Lakshmi-Vishnu on the 12th-century Khajuraho temple wall needs: the virile guardian gods who granted protection and the fearsome fertility goddesses who granted prosperity. These viras (heroes) and matas (mothers) were both powerful. Sometimes, the heroes served the loving mother. At other times, the hero controlled the wild mothers. Most times, the hero and the mother formed the perfect pair, their powers complementing each other's.

From the 5th century BCE, Buddhism along with other shramana (ascetic) movements started decrying the value placed on desire and rejected the householder's worldview. In their very monastic perspective, pleasure was frowned upon. Naturally, women, associated with pleasure and the household, became 'daughters of Mara', Mara being the demon of desire. Women were, however, admitted into monastic orders so that, through meditation and ascetic practices, they could, in their next life, acquire a male body, and achieve nirvana.

The popularity of Buddhism and other shramana orders forced Hinduism to redefine itself. The new Hinduism, based on the Puranas, put great value on desire, on household, hence relationships between men and women. In this new Hinduism, God was no longer formless; it acquired form. But neither the male nor the female form was given preference. God was seen as male: Shiva was ishwar (the lord) and Vishnu was bhagavan (all encompassing), but these male forms of the divine owed their divinity to their female counterparts. This is why both are addressed as 'husbands of the Goddess'. Shiva is Uma-pati (husband of Uma) and Vishnu is Lakshmi-vallabha (beloved of Lakshmi). Male gods can be addressed only after the name of the consort is mentioned. Thus, Shiva is Uma-Mahesh and Vishnu is Lakshmi-Narayana. Devi here is not a supplement; she is a complement.

Photograph of a typical Shiva shrine with the invisible Goddess

This was the time when monotheistic religions were on the rise around the world and Goddess cults were being wiped out, following the conversion of the Roman Emperor and his Empire to Christianity. In Christianity, God was a man and his son, the saviour, was also a man. Mary, the mother of God, was but a holy vessel, untouched by mortal man, hence virgin and mother, but not Goddess. Women were no longer priestesses; those who continued to be faithful to ancient Goddess lore and rites were deemed witches and burned at the stake.

Meanwhile, in India, the feminine provided the canvas that projected the divinity of God. This is evident in a Shiva temple. What dominates the shrine is the linga-stone representing Shiva. Some scholars see it as the phallus, but devotees see it as the form of a formless divinity (linga of that which is a-linga). What keeps this linga in place is the yoni-trough below representing Gauri (another name of Uma) and what keeps it wet and dynamic is the perforated pot above representing Ganga (another wife of Shiva, junior to Gauri, in some traditions). The shrine itself is called the garbha-griha, the womb room. Whose womb? The Devi's of course. Thus Shiva is housed inside a goddess and is between two goddesses, but only he is seen, for the temple is attributed to him. Some choose to interpret this as patriarchy: the two goddesses have been shoved into the background, granted inferior positions (consort?) in the power hierarchy. Others choose to interpret this as feminism: only through Devi can God be established. Still others see this as wisdom: the Goddess withdraws so that the devotees engage with the ascetic Shiva and force him to participate in their worldly affairs, much as a mother withdraws to encourage her child to interact with strangers.

Tanjore painting of the marriage of Meenakshi

Popular representation of Meenakshi, the goddess-queen of Madurai, Tamil Nadu

The value placed on desire and sexuality and engagement with the world in this new form of Hinduism can easily be read as a direct attack on monastic Buddhism and explains the sexual imagery on Hindu temple walls. Vishnu became an enchanting man (Mohan) for women and an enchanting woman (Mohini) for men. And just as Devi domesticates the hermit Shiva, she herself is domesticated by the handsome hermit, Shankara Sundareshwara.

From Tamil temple lore comes the story of one Meenakshi of Madurai, warrior princess with three breasts, who conquers the world but loses her masculinity and her extra breast when she sees Somasundaram, as beautiful as the moon, who is none other than Shiva. In her temple today, she may be his coy bride with a parrot in one hand, but the dagger hanging on her hip indicates her once free spirit. Amongst Tamilians, a household dominated by a woman is called Madurai (temple-town of the Goddess), while a household dominated by a man is called Chidambaram (temple-town of God).

So important is the Goddess that any attempt to worship God without Goddess is discouraged violently as explained by the story of Bhringi found in Tamil temple lore. Bhringi, an ardent devotee of Shiva, paid a visit to Mount Kailas, abode of Shiva, intent on going around his lord. But Parvati stopped him. 'Shiva and I make a pair. You cannot worship him in his totality without acknowledging me. Hence you must go around both of us.' But Bhringi was determined to only go around Shiva, not Parvati. To make this impossible, Parvati sat on Shiva's left lap. Bhringi tried squeezing between them to have his way. So Parvati fused her body with Shiva's and became his left half. Determined not to include Parvati in his worship, Bhringi turned into a bee and tried to bore

Poster art of Shiva as half woman

a path between the left and right halves of Shiva's body. Peeved at his insolence, Parvati cursed Bhringi that he would lose that part of his body that emerged from the female seed. Immediately, Bhringi lost all flesh and blood and collapsed to the ground. Reduced to nothing but bones, Bhringi apologised and sang songs to the glory of the Goddess. Finally Parvati showed mercy and gave him a third leg to enable him to stand upright. He still had a skeletal frame to remind him of the importance of the Goddess.

The half-woman form of Shiva, Ardhanareshwara, does suggest equality of God and Goddess but it is not so. This half-woman form is clearly identified with Shiva. There is no corresponding half-male form of Devi. This makes sense only when we appreciate the symbolic meaning of God and Goddess as mind and nature. The mind cannot exist without nature, but nature can exist without the mind. The Puranas thus present an idea shared by evolutionary biologists. While the visible form is gendered, the idea being communicated is genderless. This was clearly an attempt to present sophisticated ideas of Upanishad-Vedanta to the laity in narrative form. Miscommunication was a very real risk.

The Puranas also reiterate that the essence of all male gods is female. But the opposite is not true. Thus when an asura attacks and the devas run to Brahma, then Vishnu, then Shiva, they are advised to release their inner strength. This emerges in female form. From Indra comes Indrani. From Vishnu comes Vaishnavi. From Varaha comes Vairahi. From Narasimha comes Narasimhi. From Kumara comes Kumari. From Vinayaka comes Vinayaki. These become the Matrikas who collectively defeat asuras. They also merge to become Durga, the supreme defender of all devas. Durga may fight battles, emulating male heroes, but at no point does she become a man.

Miniature painting of Matrikas, the female form of devas, accompanying the Goddess into battle

While apsaras (damsels) were known to seduce tapasvins (ascetics), we find stories of Vishnu himself turning into an enchantress called Mohini to seduce not just asuras but also Shiva. Thus is born their son variously named Sastha or Aiyanar.

By the 5th century CE, temples offered legitimacy to kings who, in turn, patronised the temple. Grand temple complexes became centres of commerce, craftsmanship and culture. They housed singers, musicians, performers and, most importantly, devadasis, women who were well-versed in the arts. These were very different from the secular courtesans or ganikas of yore. They got validation by being the spouse and servant of God. They offered pleasure just as the king, the other servant of God, offered protection to pilgrims who thronged these temple towns. We find this concept in temple-cities like Puri in Odisha, Tanjavur in Tamil Nadu, and Thiruvananthapuram in Kerala. During the height of summer, the devadasis of Puri Jagannath temple, known as Maharis, were encouraged to dance for the ascetic Balarama in the hope that his seduction would herald rain. Thus monasticism was associated with drought, and sensuality with fertility. Marriage of God and Goddess was critical for the prosperity of the realm. Hence the many temple marriage festivals such as the Brahmotsavam of Venkateshwara Tirupati Balaji. The popularity of Hinduism over Buddhism as the centuries passed owes much to the sensual vibrancy of the temples that overshadowed the austerity of the monasteries.

From the 7th century onwards, a new religion gained a foothold in India – Islam. It came via trade in the south and via warlords in the north. Like Christianity, it was a monotheistic religion where

Mural from Kotakkal palace, Kerala, showing Parvati, Shiva and Mohini

God was masculine, his prophet was masculine and women had a clearly defined inferior position. Islam frowned upon idol worship and its followers could not understand the use of song, dance and theatre in worship. As Muslim warlords gradually became the rulers of north and east India, Hinduism had to redefine itself once more.

Both for internal reasons (rejection of the excessive sensuality of temple devadasis) as well as external reasons (arrival of Islam), from the 10th century onwards, we see a gradual rejection of all things sensual and feminine. This is evident in the popular ballads of the Nath-jogis (vernacular of the Sanskrit yogis), followers of Matsyendra-nath and Gorakh-nath, who are always in confrontation with sensuous Tantrik sorceresses called yoginis who get their power through sex.

Far removed from the sensuous temple culture, the Nath-jogis were wandering ascetics who attributed their power to celibacy. Some jogis even destroy their genitals, which ensures the semen does not slip out of their body but instead rises up towards their head. In Tantra, this is called urdhva-retas, the upward flow of semen that grants them powers known as siddhi, by which men have the power to fly through the sky, walk on water, give fertility to the land and children to the childless. The acquisition of siddhi turned the Nath-jogis into Siddhas, powerful men who had no time to waste on sensory worldly pleasures.

The attitude of the Nath-jogi tradition towards celibacy is very different from that in Buddhist times. In Buddhist tradition, it was more about the conquest of desire. In Nath tradition, it is about the rejection of all things feminine. The Nath-jogi's hyper-masculinity did not come from dominating women; it came from turning away

Circular temple of 64 yoginis in Odisha

Painting of Vajra-yogini from the Tantrik tradition

from women altogether. Femininity was seen as stripping men of their masculinity.

Matsyendra-nath was born a fish but he overheard the secret conversation between Shiva and Shakti, during which Shiva revealed the mysteries of Vedas and the Tantras to Parvati. That knowledge transformed him into a human male with enough siddhi power to enter the banana grove unharmed. He entered this land of women and stayed there, enchanted by the women, unable to return. He had to be rescued by his student, Gorakh-nath.

Even the story of the great Vedanta teacher Shankara has these elements when challenged about his knowledge of the erotic arts by Ubhaya Bharati, wife of Mandana Mishra. Since he is a celibate ascetic, Shankara knows nothing, so he resurrects a dead king, Amaru, by entering his body at the moment of his death and then going on to experience sensory pleasures in the inner quarters of the palace with queens and courtesans for several months. Unlike Mastyendra-nath, however, Shankara does not succumb to the pleasures of the flesh and eventually leaves the king's body and returns to being an ascetic, thus establishing the superiority of his mind over his flesh.

Alongside violent Muslim warlords came the poet-saints known as Sufis from Persia. With them came music and the idea of love for God expressed in passionate, even romantic terms. Hindus connected with this idea and it amplified the bhakti or devotional movement.

The idea of devotion is found in the *Bhagavad Gita* written centuries before the rise of Islam. Tamil songs of Alvars and

Miniature painting of Radha and Krishna

Nayanars that speak of devotion to Vishnu and Shiva predate the arrival of Islam into India. But the tone of devotion here is one of surrender. The arrival of Sufism made devotion more romantic. It also encouraged the expression of devotion through regional literature.

Indian poets took the idea of romantic attachment for the divine to another level through the idea of Radha. Krishna had always been associated with milkmaids who yearn for him, but in the songs of the poet-saints, Krishna also pines for Radha and Radha demands and gets Krishna's attention. It is no longer about submission; it is now about mutual longing. The devotee becomes a woman, a maid, a servant, even a wife and a queen who God indulges with affection.

Those who could not handle the romantic and the sensual turned to the parental. But it was not always God who was the parent. The devotee could be parent too: Yashoda to Krishna and Kaushalya to Ram.

Most early bhakti songs were directed at Vishnu and Shiva. Later bhakti songs are directed at the Goddess too. Shyama Sangeet in Bengal and the Jagrata songs sung all night for the pleasure of Sheravali in Punjab and Jammu, for example. The relationship here is never romantic. It is always parental. Here the Goddess is mostly mother. At times she appears like a daughter, virginal and powerful, rarely mischievous and playful. In Sri Vaishnavism, strongly influenced by the teachings of Ramanuja, the 12th century Vedantic scholar who turned away from married life and became a monk, Shri or Lakshmi is the mother who the devotee approaches so that she will negotiate with the stern father, Vishnu.

In Sufi songs, God is decidedly male, and the male singer-

Gopeshwara Mahadeva of Mathura represents Shiva who became a gopi in order to dance with Krishna.

Popular image of Vinayaki, the shakti of Ganesha, who is visualised in female form.

Painting of Srinathji who is Krishna, showing him in sakhi-vesha, or the costume of a lady friend.

Gods embracing the feminine

devotee does not shy away from making himself feminine. In Bhakti literature, this gender shifting extends to God. Love for the devotee turns the masculine into feminine and the feminine into masculine.

In Trichy, Tamil Nadu, Shiva turns into a midwife in order to help deliver the child of a devotee whose mother is unable to reach her house in time. In Mathura, Shiva turns into a gopeshwara, a milkmaid, who wants to join Krishna in his raas-leela.

Krishna exchanges clothes with Radha to experience what it means to be Radha. And in imagery found on temple walls of Odisha, he does not mind sporting a woman's plait and anklets. In his Nathdvara temple in Rajasthan, he indulges in stri-vesha, or cross-dressing, in memory of his mother and his beloved, unafraid that such activities will undermine his masculinity.

There is an oral tradition in Bengal about a time that came when Kali's violence became so excessive that the world lost its balance. She had to be stopped. So Shiva lay on his back, on the ground, in her path. As soon as she stepped on him, she was so enchanted by his beauty that her strident march came to a halt and she decided to make love to him, with her on top. With this, the balance of the world was restored and the earth regenerated itself. But then the asuras returned. The devas begged Kali to come to their rescue and rid the earth of asuras. But Kali was so full of love that she could not resume her violence. So she decided to take another form, that of Krishna. From female, she became male. Shiva could not bear the thought of being without Kali so he decided to follow Krishna as Radha. Krishna was as dark as Kali and Radha was as fair as Shiva. Kali had sat on top of Shiva and so Krishna allowed Radha to sit on top of him. Thus their respective gender and positions

Odisha patta painting of a composite image of Krishna and Kali were reversed. Krishna was Kali. Shiva was Radha. They were not two but one.

By worshipping Krishna then, one did not exclude Kali. And by worshipping Radha, one did not exclude Shiva. The gender fluidity of the narrative seeks to unite Vaishnava, Shaiva and Shakta orders. It allows for negotiations and interactions between the vegetarian Krishna cults and the non-vegetarian Kali cults. It also unites the ascetic Shaiva traditions with the sensuous Radha traditions.

When there is wisdom, there is affection. When there is affection, there is no fear of predators, hence no need for boundaries. Rigidity then gives way to fluidity: God becomes Goddess and Goddess, God.

In the 16th century, Europeans came to India as traders. By the 18th century, they had complete control over the subcontinent, turning this land into a source of taxes as well as raw materials for their industries back home. The Europeans had Christian roots and saw themselves as children of the enlightenment who came with a scientific temperament. They mocked Hindus for being so 'effeminate' and described Hinduism as paganism as they worshipped the Goddess.

Hindus reacted by masculinising themselves, distancing themselves from all things sensual, and redefining the Goddess in virginal and maternal terms, just like the biblical Mary. All things Hindu were seen as foul. So rather than reform devdasi traditions of their exploitative side, they were simply wiped out, and all dance and song sanitised. Freedom fighters projected themselves

Twin goddesses who are autonomous, without male companionship as celibate monks more determined to serve Mother India as yogis. They refused to be seen as rasiks and bhogis who enjoyed art and pleasure.

The impact of the European Orientalist gaze was so powerful that it continues to haunt modern political Hinduism where leaders are especially respected if they are celibate. Posters have been created of Ram without Sita and Shiva without Gauri, both sporting firm muscular bodies with determined expressions, and no trace of feminine softness. Durga, the protective mother who rides lions and does battle, has become the preferred form of the Goddess, not Kamakshi, who sits on Shiva holding the symbols of Kama, god of desire, or the restless whimsical Lakshmi.

The 20th century saw the rise of American academia. It had two powerful influences. One was the Protestant rejection of Catholic feudalism, even though it still remained masculine and monotheistic at its core. The other was scientific thinking that rejected all matters of faith. It established a neo-Orientalist lens that started explaining Hinduism through the lens of fairness and justice, where it positioned the researcher as the saviour and the research subject either as villain or victim. Suddenly, the Ramayana and Mahabharata became patriarchal epics. The differences between many Ramayanas were more valued than the commonalities. The Ram of devotees was no longer the gentle God but the stern imperialist, a wife-abusing villain, and Sita became his whimpering silent victim, stripped of her Goddess status. This reading was reinforced when Ram became the mascot of Hindu fundamentalism. Shiva was admired as the rule-breaker who allows the wild Kali to stand on his chest, while Vishnu was frowned upon because he makes Lakshmi a subservient consort

The difference between Western and Indian gaze

who has to massage his feet. This literal and rather rudimentary reading shaped by Western ideologies and templates continues to have a huge impact on young students who go to American universities to pursue studies in humanities and liberal arts. It endorses the Western imagination that there is nothing redeeming about India: it is essentially chaos where order has to be brought in from outside; its many hierarchies have to be replaced by equality; and it is desperately in need of a Western-style revolution.

The Goddess smiles. It is in the nature of the beast to compete and dominate. Like young lions who challenge old ones, like dogs who bark at strangers, every society mocks older alien cultures. The West is no different, despite the veneer of rationality and science. And like animals who do not recognise themselves in the mirror, societies often fail to see themselves as others see them. India is no different when they turn chauvinistic.

Vitthai asks: what is wrong with gods being feminine and men being effeminate? Why should women be like men? Why should there be a race that someone has to win? Why can't people be themselves? The nature of man cannot be domesticated by rules that enforce fairness and justice. Such rules will only suppress and eventually provoke the beast within humanity to strike back, defy and subvert the very same laws. For what starts as a tool to create equality invariably ends up as a tool that establishes new hierarchies.

The Goddess has seen it before and she will see it again. As long as Brahma seeks to control nature, he will find himself being beheaded by Shiva. As long as Indra believes he is entitled to Lakshmi, he will always wonder why she is drawn to Vishnu.

The point is not about domesticating the Goddess outside

Clay image from Bengal of Jaga-dhatri, the mother of the world us; the point is to evoke the God within us. It is not about being righteous, about proving the validity of one God or one truth; it is about expanding the mind so that we can affectionately include multiple truths. And that can only happen when we appreciate that idea that is Goddess, hence God, without the bias of gender.

Acknowledgements

I would like to thank all those who helped in the making of the book including:

- Satya Banerjee for giving me access to his vast collection of Goddess images and permission to use them.
- Ayan Chaudhuri for his photograph of Durga.
- Pramod Kumar K G for giving me access to rare images from his library.
- Dhaivat Chhaya and Swapnil Sakpal for designing the book and helping with the artwork.